T0010627

Living a Committed Life

Living a Committed Life

Finding Freedom and Fulfillment in a Purpose Larger Than Yourself

LYNNE TWIST

with Mary Earle Chase

BK

Berrett–Koehler Publishers, Inc.

Copyright © 2023 by Lynne Twist

All rights reserved. No part of this publication may be reproduced, distributed, or transmitted in any form or by any means, including photocopying, recording, or other electronic or mechanical methods, without the prior written permission of the publisher, except in the case of brief quotations embodied in critical reviews and certain other noncommercial uses permitted by copyright law. For permission requests, write to the publisher, addressed "Attention: Permissions Coordinator," at the address below.

Berrett-Koehler Publishers, Inc. Tel: (510) 817-2277
1333 Broadway, Suite 1000 Fax: (510) 817-2278
Oakland, CA 94612-1921 www.bkconnection.com

Ordering Information
Quantity sales. Special discounts are available on quantity purchases by corporations, associations, and others. For details, contact the "Special Sales Department" at the Berrett-Koehler address above.
Individual sales. Berrett-Koehler publications are available through most bookstores. They can also be ordered directly from Berrett-Koehler: Tel: (800) 929-2929; Fax: (802) 864-7626; www.bkconnection.com.
Orders for college textbook/course adoption use. Please contact Berrett-Koehler: Tel: (800) 929-2929; Fax: (802) 864-7626.

Distributed to the U.S. trade and internationally by Penguin Random House Publisher Services.

Berrett-Koehler and the BK logo are registered trademarks of Berrett-Koehler Publishers, Inc.

Printed in the United States of America

Berrett-Koehler books are printed on long-lasting acid-free paper. When it is available, we choose paper that has been manufactured by environmentally responsible processes. These may include using trees grown in sustainable forests, incorporating recycled paper, minimizing chlorine in bleaching, or recycling the energy produced at the paper mill.

Library of Congress Cataloging-in-Publication Data
Names: Twist, Lynne, author. | Chase, Mary Earle, 1945- author.
Title: Living a committed life : finding freedom and fulfillment in a
    purpose larger than yourself / Lynne Twist, with Mary Earle Chase.
Description: First edition. | Oakland, CA : Berrett-Koehler Publishers, Inc.,
    [2023] | Includes index.
Identifiers: LCCN 2022013985 (print) | LCCN 2022013986 (ebook) |
    ISBN 9781523093090 (paperback) | ISBN 9781523093106 (pdf) |
    ISBN 9781523093113 (epub) | ISBN 9781523093120
Subjects: LCSH: Commitment (Psychology) | Conduct of life. | Social action. | Social change.
Classification: LCC BF619 .T95 2023 (print) | LCC BF619 (ebook) | DDC
    158—dc23/eng/20220615
LC record available at https://lccn.loc.gov/2022013985
LC ebook record available at https://lccn.loc.gov/2022013986

First Edition
28 27 26 25 24 23   10 9 8 7 6 5 4 3 2 1

Book producer: Linda Jupiter Productions Proofreader: Mary Kanable
Editor: Elissa Rabellino Indexer: Lieser Indexing
Text designer: Kim Scott, Bumpy Design Cover designer: Nita Ybarra

DEDICATED TO

The love of my life, Bill Twist

CONTENTS

FOREWORD

by Van Jones

M any years ago, when I met Lynne Twist, I knew that the way she lived her life was unusual and inspiring, something to pay attention to. At the time, having graduated from Yale Law School, I was a young lawyer who had chosen to apply my skills and experience toward fixing our broken prison system. It was daunting work, and I knew I needed to stay connected to people who would keep me motivated and inspired. I needed allies who knew the harsh realities of the world but who kept their visions and commitment intact. Over the past decades, Lynne has been one of those people for me. With this remarkable book, she will do the same for you.

Lynne has continued to be a powerful friend and mentor, supporting me on my own path of living a committed life. I experience the privilege of turning my life over to serving the highest good, and I feel the freedom and fulfillment she speaks of so eloquently on these pages. Lynne's life work has taken her throughout the world and given her access to some of the most extraordinary people on the planet. The stories she shares from these encounters and her own amazing life will touch your heart and even make you weep, but more importantly they will inspire you to step more fully into your own self-expression.

The times we are living in call for you to step up, to find your own path to contributing to the radical transformation that is needed now. As Lynne says, humanity needs to make an evolutionary leap—not merely to sustain life, but to truly regenerate all of our human and natural systems. The mindset and principles that have guided her life are applicable to all of us and will strengthen our capacity to be ever more effective in making a difference with who we are and the gifts we've been given.

Lynne reminds us that each of us has a role to play in these challenging times. We may think we are ordinary, but it is a commitment, a stand for something larger than ourselves, that shapes our lives and makes us extraordinary. Breakdowns and breakthroughs are abundant in a committed life, and I'm honored that Lynne shares a couple of stories of my process in this book.

If you haven't found your own calling, this book will motivate and inspire you to discover it and put it into action. If you are already living a committed life, the chapters that follow will affirm the path you've chosen and will strengthen and empower you. *Living a Committed Life* holds the keys to the kingdom of inspired action at a time when nothing is more important than a breakthrough for humanity.

VAN JONES *is an Emmy Award–winning news and political commentator, as well as an attorney, best-selling author, and changemaker. He is the cofounder of several social justice and environmental organizations and is a recipient of Jeff Bezos's inaugural Courage and Civility Award, along with many other honors and awards. His official website is* vanjones.net.

A Committed Life

Until one is committed, there is hesitancy, the chance to draw back, always ineffectiveness. Concerning all acts of initiative (and creation), there is one elementary truth, the ignorance of which kills countless ideas and splendid plans: that the moment one definitely commits oneself, then Providence moves too. All sorts of things occur to help one that would never otherwise have occurred. A whole stream of events issues from the decision, raising in one's favour all manner of unforeseen incidents and meetings and material assistance, which no man could have dreamt would have come his way. I have learned a deep respect for one of Goethe's couplets:

Whatever you can do, or dream you can, begin it.
Boldness has genius, power, and magic in it!

—WILLIAM HUTCHISON MURRAY

I t's February 1977. I remember everything about that moment in time: a generic meeting room; sitting in the back row on the left side of the room, dressed up in a green plaid shirt and what I thought were some really cool pants. In the front of the room was Werner Erhard, the founder of the Erhard Seminars Training, known as *est*, and between us were about 60 VIPs, including members of the est Advisory Board. I was assisting at this event, which meant taking care of the room and hosting the attendees, who included international business leaders, top university professors, and celebrities like John Denver.

Werner announced to the group, "I'm committing myself to ending world hunger and to generating an environment where millions of people can make that commitment. I'm going to make it part of what the est graduates have the opportunity to participate in. This will be a focus of the est organization, and because we don't have a name for it, we'll call it, temporarily, The Hunger Project."

There was a stunned silence in the room as Werner continued. He held up his hand as he described what he called the front and the back side of the hand of hunger. "The front side of the hand of hunger is the physical hunger—the starvation, the malnutrition, the malabsorptive hunger—but the back side of the hand of hunger is the hunger for meaning in the well-fed world, the hunger to make a difference with our lives. These two are related, and we're going to end that whole hunger, both the front and the back side of the hand of hunger. That's what The Hunger Project will do."

All of a sudden, I was in tears; I could barely catch my breath. At that moment, I knew that I was going to be involved in this project. I thought, "This is why I'm on this planet now; this is my life's work."

Then the pushback from the group of advisers began, and there were strong objections: "What are you talking about, Werner? Have you lost your mind? You can't end hunger. You can't say that publicly; this is completely too much. We've put our reputations on the line to legitimize the est training, and this is going to completely blow it for all of us."

As the objections and outrage continued, I found myself remembering when I was a little girl of five with my family barbecuing in the backyard of our home. My mom said (as so many mothers have said), "Eat your hamburger, clean your plate. There are children starving in Korea."

I asked her about Korea, because she had grown up there, and she told me, "Yes, there are children like you, your age, who don't eat for days. They don't have food or sometimes even water." I couldn't believe it; I was just incredulous that there were children going hungry.

And I said to myself then, "When I grow up, I'm going to do something about that."

So, sitting there in that est meeting amid the noise and rancor, I felt a strange peace: "This is why I'm sitting here. This is who I am. Ending hunger is what my life is about."

I was turning 32 years old, and I had discovered a path in life I had never imagined: a commitment so huge it would completely transform my life. I gave up being a comfortable full-time wife and mother to devote myself to the end of hunger and starvation by the end of the century. This mission completely captivated me for two decades as I traveled the world and raised many millions of dollars for The Hunger Project. I realized that the purpose of my life is to make a difference: to leave the planet better than I found it.

I came to see that I could live what I call "a committed life," which is a life governed not by my desires, by my wants, or even by my needs, but rather by what I'm committed to. And I discovered that commitment is not a burden but a liberation. I was actually liberated by having a purpose larger than my own life. I was freed from my petty thoughts of not being worthy and from my doubts and fears about whether or not people liked me. All that fell away, and my commitment really took me over. By turning over my life to service, I found that I didn't have to make a lot of decisions and try to figure out if I was doing things right or wrong. Somehow, I could feel in my body what to do and how to be. Something wants to happen, and I am the vehicle.

MY COMMITTED LIFE

Once I experienced being a conduit for something larger than myself, I began to sense the world in a new way. Standing in my lifetime commitment to ending hunger, I felt I could sense what wanted to happen. The world opened up to me in new ways, and the most challenging issues of our time began to call to me. Since then, a succession of new opportunities have come my way that have shaped my committed life.

After nearly two decades of work for The Hunger Project, I also became involved with the leadership of the State of the World Forum, a multiyear gathering of global leaders in San Francisco to plan for the success of humanity in the new millennium. In these groundbreaking gatherings, held annually between 1995 through 1999, I associated with many of the world's most transformative leaders, including Mikhail Gorbachev, Jane Goodall, Jacques Cousteau, Betty Friedan, Carl Sagan, and many others.

At about this same time, in an extraordinary and mystical experience, I was called in dreams by an Indigenous tribe in the Amazon rainforest to assist them in protecting their territory from oil exploitation. My husband, Bill Twist, and I, along with our friend John Perkins, created a partnership with them called the Pachamama Alliance, which has become a global movement not only for saving the Amazon rainforest but also for activating people's commitment to a just, sustainable, and fulfilling future.

Seeing how the fundamental misconception of scarcity on this abundant planet is at the root of all of our global crises, I was called to speak out for a vision of a world based on sufficiency. There is enough to go around, and we no longer live in a you or me world; rather, we are called to a *you and me* world—a world that works for everyone, with no one and nothing left out. This vision led to my first book, *The Soul of Money: Transforming Your Relationship with Money and Life*, and to the formation of the Soul of Money Institute, offering training in Fundraising from the Heart as well as transformative courses for women seeking to make a difference with their lives.

My commitment to empowering women and girls began with my work with The Hunger Project and expanded over the years. I have been blessed to collaborate with the Nobel Women's Initiative in their work of reducing the impact of war and violence on women worldwide. These female Nobel Peace Prize winners have exposed me to life-changing experiences and inspired me with the depth and breadth of their commitments. As we entered the 21st century, I became more focused on the role of women in creating the future we want. I began to refer to these times as the Sophia Century, a crucial era in which women will take their rightful place in coequal partnership with men, and the world will come into balance.

All of my commitments, sourced from my overarching stand
for a world that works for everyone, have given me an extraordinary life of connection to great human beings, to great conversations, to causes and groups that are making a historic difference
in the evolution of humankind. I have traveled the world and
had remarkable adventures on six continents. Although at first
my husband and children were stunned at the depth of my commitment—and suffered some neglect as a result—over time,
they joined me, and we became a whole family committed to
contributing to a new future.

A PURPOSE LARGER THAN YOURSELF

For the purposes of this book, *commitment* means dedication
to a cause or purpose larger than yourself. As we well know,
people can be committed primarily to themselves and their own
causes—a business, the family, a sport or hobby. In fact, that is
where most people place their devotion and loyalty. You can live
a life dedicated to mothering or gardening or making money,
but I am asking that you consider a commitment to the com-
mon good: to something that takes you out of yourself and into
the realm of service.

Living a committed life is not about doing good so that you
can feel good about yourself or look good to others. It is about
answering a call that creates a new context for your life. Living this way is guided by taking a stand and giving your word
that you will live into that stand and have it shape your life. It
requires keeping that commitment in the face of challenges by
creating a context of possibility and transformation. You learn
to pay attention, to train yourself to navigate the upsets and
challenges and to learn from and be nourished by them.

When you are able to turn breakdowns into breakthroughs, then whatever comes at you in life (a job loss, a death, cancer, the breakup of a marriage) can become a gift; it's all there to teach you, to empower you somehow. You're freed from falling into the dark hole of depression or wallowing in jealousy or envy. It's not that life's difficulties don't show up, but they show up in a way that you are served by them rather than being taken down by them. That's the frame of reference that I come from. I can't prove if this is universally true or false; I just know that it works. This mindset is what has allowed me to discover the distinct joys of living a committed life.

OUR TIMES CALL FOR COMMITMENT

I offer my vision of a committed life because the times we live in are calling for it. We are in a new era where the very survival of humanity and myriad other life forms is called into question. Having altered the composition of the planet's atmosphere with ever-growing concentrations of greenhouse gases, having warmed the oceans and poisoned them with pollutants and plastics, having caused the extinction of unknown numbers of plants and animals—we have to admit that we as a species are pretty darn powerful. If we can create these massive changes, we can also stop them. But to do so will take many millions of us living purposeful lives: lives of commitment to the future rather than to our own comfort and desires.

Our dreams of a future where we could have meaningful work and also relax, play, and maybe even roam this beautiful planet now seem elusive. The existential nature of our global crises (worldwide pandemics, global warming, species extinction, runaway inequality) means that much more is required of us. We can transform our fear and anxiety into commitment and action. That transformation is what interrupts and heals the fear, and it moves the dial on what is causing it.

In facing the dark shadows showing up in our polarized politics (racism, sexism, militarism), we have to confront our own darkness and heal our own hearts. So, in committing to a vision, a purpose larger than our own lives, we are freed from the smallness and pettiness of our own minds and catapulted out of anxiety and fear into inspired action. Rather than putting all of our energy into trying to protect what we have, we can focus our imagination and our efforts on re-creating and regenerating all of our human systems for the next phase of our evolution. There's never been a time when we needed inspired action more than now.

We humans are poised to make an evolutionary leap. That's why I have included in this book stories related to the arenas of commitment that I believe are crucial to our future. If you are looking for where to focus your talent and energy, consider taking on ending hunger and poverty, changing the destructive dream of the modern world, generating effective action on reversing global warming, empowering women and girls, or contributing to creating a more inclusive, fair, and ecological economy. There's so much to be done, urgently, but there is still time, and we can do it.

It is easy to slip into denial, depression, or hopelessness about the future. Yes, we face an uncertain future: yet what a time to be alive! What we do collectively in the coming years will determine the future of the planet for perhaps thousands of years to come. That may sound daunting, overwhelming, or even burdensome. But my experience is that this view ennobles our lives and gives us the opportunity to live the most meaningful lives any generation has ever had.

If you are already committed to a life of service, this book aims to validate and support you. If you are longing to find where to serve—to have your talents used for a purpose larger than yourself—I hope this book will inspire and guide you. In sharing the perspective gained in my decades on this planet, I often say that I don't have answers, but I do have stories. In my world travels and life as a pro-activist, I've had extraordinary experiences with extraordinary people, and I share them for the lessons they might convey and for the insights they may provoke in you.

So, while I hope you enjoy and are moved by the stories I share here, my deepest intention is to inspire and motivate you to look inside yourself for your own commitments—to ponder your own role in creating the future you want for yourself and for future generations. What is your role to play? It may be a big role, or it may be a small role, but if you play it, your life can have a meaning beyond what you have dreamed of. Living a committed life will bring you an experience of great freedom and profound fulfillment, as well as unimaginable joy.

PART I

The Power of Commitment

Making a commitment to a purpose larger than yourself
has the power not only to give your life meaning
but to make a difference at a time when humanity
faces the greatest challenges we've ever known.

CHAPTER I

A Splendid Torch

*This is the true joy in life, the being used for a purpose
recognized by yourself as a mighty one . . . the being a force
of Nature instead of a feverish selfish little clod of ailments
and grievances complaining that the world will not devote
itself to making you happy. I am of the opinion that my
life belongs to the whole community, and as long as I live,
it is my privilege to do for it whatever I can. I want to
be thoroughly used up when I die, for the harder I work,
the more I live. I rejoice in life for its own sake. Life is
no brief candle to me. It is a sort of splendid torch which
I've got a hold of for the moment, and I want to make it
burn as brightly as possible before handing it on to future
generations.*

—GEORGE BERNARD SHAW

This quote from the British writer and activist has been framed on our mantel for decades and says in a few lines what I hope to convey in this book. For me, it epitomizes the meaning of commitment. Over the years, I have seen my own "selfish little clod of ailments and grievances" disappear as I devoted myself to a higher calling. I've aimed to live my life as a splendid torch lighting the way for future generations.

I've known many people who have held that torch, but the person who most epitomizes that kind of commitment for me is the renowned inventor and visionary Buckminster Fuller, one of the great geniuses of the 20th century. Bucky, as he was called, became a friend and a mentor, and although he died in 1983, his ideas and insights inspire me to this day.

In 1976, a friend invited me to an event called an Integrity Day, where Buckminster Fuller spoke to an audience of 2,000 people. A small man wearing thick glasses and dressed in a black suit, he stood onstage behind a table of models of his "tensegrity" structures (tetrahedrons, octahedrons, and icosahedrons) that were the basis of his famous geodesic domes. Bucky was talking about the intellectual integrity of the universe, and I didn't really understand much of what he was saying, but I got who he was. As the Emerson quote says so beautifully, "Who you are speaks so loudly, I can't hear the words you're saying." That was my experience of Bucky Fuller.

At a certain point, he stepped out from behind the table, looked out into the audience, and said, "Now I'm going to say the most important thing I've ever said, or perhaps ever will say. Humanity has just passed a critical threshold. We are doing so much more with so much less that we now live in a world where there is enough, enough for everyone to live a healthy and productive life."

Sitting in the audience, I could feel my heart pounding and my eyes filled with tears as I listened to this exuberant and eloquent man speaking about what it would take to create "a world that works for everyone, with no one and nothing left out." He fervently believed that this was possible, that humanity already possessed the resources and technology to meet the needs of everyone on the planet. For me, Bucky smashed the myth of scarcity, that there is not enough to go around. He introduced the notion that we are on the verge of replacing a *you or me* world, one of competition for scarce resources, with a *you and me* world, one of sufficiency for all. With these words, he planted in me the vision that would soon become the guiding force of my life. I was blown away by his revolutionary and transformational vision of the world and our human future, and I had a visceral, physical, spiritual, out-of-time experience, the realization that my life would never be the same.

BUCKMINSTER FULLER'S STORY

Nearly 80 years old at this time, Bucky told the story of his own personal transformation, an epiphany that I consider to be one of those magical moments that changed the world. In 1927, at the age of 32, he was grieving the loss of his four-year-old daughter some years before as well as the loss of the business that was his livelihood. Another child was on the way, and he had no savings and no prospects for supporting his family. He was drinking heavily and characterized himself as a "throwaway human being."

One afternoon in Chicago, walking around Lake Michigan, he contemplated suicide by drowning so that his family could receive his life insurance. Suddenly he felt himself suspended above the ground in a sphere of white light, and a voice spoke, telling him, "You do not belong to you. You belong to the Universe, and your role is to apply yourself to converting your experiences to the highest advantage of others." From that moment forward, Bucky devoted himself to what he called an experiment: "to find what a single individual could contribute to changing the world and benefiting all humanity."

Bucky was the first example I had known of a person who had turned his life over to a purpose larger than himself and who helped me discover the possibility of living a committed life. Key to Bucky's message was the power of an ordinary human being, what he called a "little individual," to make a difference that would impact all humanity. Bucky did indeed give his extraordinary gifts to the planet as, in his words, a "comprehensive anticipatory design scientist" to solve global problems. His work as an architect, systems theorist, author, designer, inventor, and futurist still inspires and challenges people of all generations. He is indeed a splendid torch for me and millions of others.

There is more to come about Bucky as my mentor and family friend. I introduce him here as a way to examine the nature of commitment. There are many ways to look at the word, the idea, and the concept. For the purposes of this book, commitment is giving your word—not only giving your word, but being consistent with your word. The etymology of the word—pledging oneself—means you become the commitment you've made. Commitment is an act of courage, integrity, and boldness. A profound commitment is a declaration of the soul of who you are and what you're up to in this lifetime. It could possibly be the most powerful action a person can take. I've seen that with my own eyes; I've lived that with my own life.

COMMITMENT AS A CONTEXT FOR LIFE

In the conversation that is this book, you will see and experience how giving one's word from a place of authenticity and courage can be life-altering and life-defining. A bold, audacious commitment can shape every action you take. It's not a decision and not merely an agreement; it becomes the context of your life. Commitment is especially powerful when connected to the needs of the world that touch your heart. It enables you to take your grievances and your heartache about the world and do something about it. The very words "I commit" can stir the soul of both the one who speaks them and those who hear them. I've found that making commitment public enough that the people you respect, love, and trust hold you to account is empowering. Then people relate to you not as your desires, your personality, or your agenda, but rather as your word. They interact with the integrity of the commitment you've made.

A commitment larger than your own wants and needs lifts you out of the landscape of your circumstances and personal desires. It lifts you out of day-to-day moods, irritations, and upsets about things not going your way. It pulls you out of that smallness and elevates you to a place where you find the strength and courage to generate your life out of possibility and generosity.

All great movements, all major alterations in the course of history, began with a courageous commitment by a human being who said what they meant and meant what they said—someone who held themselves accountable to a standard beyond what they knew possible of themselves. For me, once the commitment to end world hunger was spoken, a new domain of existence was born. When President John F. Kennedy committed to getting a man on the moon within nine years, a whole new field of aeronautics and space science was born—along with national inspiration and aspiration. When a small group of men and women in England committed to ending slavery, they began a worldwide revolution. When Mahatma Gandhi said the British would walk out of India and India would be independent, an unstoppable, nonviolent movement was born.

That kind of commitment is born of the heart, from the soul, from the deepest place of who we are. It comes from what some of us call God, Spirit, or Source, and it is equally felt by any-one who is moved to hear a calling from life itself. It's an act of courage, which comes from the heart. What I'm talking about isn't logical. It doesn't come from the mind. It's not irrational or rational. It's not even in that domain. I call it *trans-rational*—in the domain of transformation. It changes the game, moves the world, and creates a space for miracles.

People often think that great leaders are born, not made—that they are somehow destined for greatness. I believe, however, it's the opposite—that committing oneself to an inspiring cause is what forges you into a great human being. It's the commit-ment that shapes you into who you need to be to fulfill it. And that's the point of this book. It's not that you have to be smart enough or talented enough or knowledgeable enough to make commitments. You make the commitment, and then the talent, the knowledge, the passion, the resources start to become visi-ble and move toward you. The light of a splendid torch attracts them to you. When something greater calls you, human frail-ties—which we all have—begin to fall away or move into the background. Instead of focusing only on your own wants and needs, you put your attention on the larger community—what Shaw called the "true joy in life."

People who've made a big commitment seem larger than life, but they didn't start out like that. Gandhi was a small man who was thrown off the train in South Africa and became a huge hero for generations to come. Jane Goodall went to Africa as a young researcher before she had any scientific credentials, yet her relationship with chimpanzees gave scientists and the rest of us a completely new perspective on primate behavior. Greta Thunberg was a young girl on the autism spectrum who got very angry about inaction on climate change and just started sitting outside the Swedish Parliament instead of going to classes. She took her anger and transformed it into a beacon of light so powerful that she mobilized millions and millions of young people to join in climate action. Even people living in downtrodden circumstances where it looks like there's no hope have found deep commitment. Cesar Chavez is such a beautiful example. He spent every day of many years toiling in fields and picking grapes with no rest, no health care, no decent wages or place to live. But something happened that sparked his commitment. And then he started to live by that commitment, and the farmworkers' movement was born.

The possibility of that kind of commitment, I declare, lives in everyone—everyone who's alive, or they wouldn't be here. Many people live their lives without ever tapping into it or even getting close to it, but we are all capable of living committed lives, and I want to make sure it is accessible to everyone.

I have been blessed to have a privileged life that afforded me the opportunity to follow my passion, and for that I am beyond grateful. However, I have seen that a committed life is not a function of circumstances—that jobs and families need not define service. Raising children is obviously a massive investment of time and commitment and might seem a deterrent to substantial broader contribution. During the long battle for women's right to vote, some leaders, like Susan B. Anthony, had no children, while others, like Elizabeth Cady Stanton, had eight children to raise, yet they all worked together side by side. For some, it was totally inconvenient, while others had all the time in the world, yet they both stepped up. I am particularly inspired by mothers who have lived a committed life. For example, among the women Nobel Peace Prize winners who make up the Nobel Women's Initiative, Leymah Gbowee, a freedom fighter from Liberia, has six children. Tawakkol Karman, an exiled journalist from Yemen, has three children, and she's still fighting for human rights in her country.

Often, heroes and heroines who have lived committed lives are unknown and unacknowledged. I think of the fathers and mothers whose commitment to their children made astonishing contributions to society, even under the harshest of circumstances. Berdis Jane Baldwin raised her son James and eight other children as a single mother working as a domestic servant. Louise Langdon Little, the mother of Malcolm X, had eight children who went to foster homes after she was involuntarily institutionalized for "believing she was being discriminated against." Martin Luther King Jr.'s mother, Alberta Williams King, was murdered six years after her son was assassinated. She was shot in the back while playing piano in Ebenezer Baptist Church. These women were directly responsible for the empowerment of their children as well as the entire Black community.

WHEN ORDINARY PEOPLE
BECOME EXTRAORDINARY

Ordinary people become extraordinary when they take a stand for a purpose larger than themselves. I have witnessed extraordinary leadership arising from people in every circumstance and culture on earth. One, who is very dear to me, is Narcisa Mashienta, an Indigenous woman from the Ecuadorean Amazon. She was originally from the Shuar people but had been married at a young age to an Achuar man and lived in the tiny community of Pumpuentsa, deep in a remote area of the Amazon rainforest. As part of a dream culture, Narcisa had had dreams throughout her childhood that she would play a leadership role in that part of the forest, but there had never been a woman leader in the community; it was almost forbidden.

At the age of 19, she encountered the Pachamama Alliance, which was bringing committed activists from the United States and Europe into Achuar territory, a region of the Amazon rainforest still roadless and untouched by extractive industries. Margaret Love, a nurse and midwife from Berkeley, California, had visited the Achuar a few times and discovered that their birthing practices were dangerous for both mother and baby. When a woman was ready to give birth, she went off into the forest by herself. With no one attending, she lay on banana leaves on the ground and tied herself to a stake in the ground that she could hold on to while squatting and pushing. She would cut the umbilical cord herself with a special, very sharp tool made of bamboo, which was actually fairly hygienic.

The women made the best of this birthing practice, but too often, women and babies died—breech babies, stillbirths, mothers hemorrhaging to death. The women of Sharamentsa village, learning that Margaret was a nurse and a midwife, asked for her help. When Margaret inquired about who might spearhead the project locally, Narcisa—young, intelligent, and charismatic—was everyone's recommendation.

Narcisa was well aware of these constant birthing tragedies. Her tribe, the Shuar, had safer birthing practices, but Narcisa, being young and of a different tribe, felt she had no power to advocate for change. She found an ally in Margaret, whose medical training gave her some clout with the Achuar. Narcisa stepped up and committed to partnering with her to discover how they might transform childbearing into a safe and healthy process with support from the community. Together they brought into existence a local community health program called Ikiama Nukuri, which in Achuar means "women as keepers of the forest." Walking, sometimes for days, in the forest to reach surrounding communities, they began recruiting women to be trained to work in their own villages. In this traditional warrior culture, Ikiama Nukuri was the first opportunity these women experienced to have a say in their lives.

Narcisa became the director of Ikiama Nukuri and has made it an unqualified success. Within eight years, 100 percent of unnecessary deaths of mothers and children were stopped. The program has expanded throughout Achuar and Schuar territories, providing communities with safe birthing kits as well as addressing other community health concerns. Although it took several years, eventually the Achuar men began supporting the project as well.

Ikiama Nukuri has also become the source of a surprising rise of leadership among the Indigenous women, who now hold elected positions in local governance and are engaged with national and international advocacy. Narcisa has given a talk at a TEDx event in Quito, Ecuador; spoken at Columbia Business School in New York City; and traveled to international climate conferences. True to her earlier dreams, she has become a leader —a humble, profoundly respected, and sought-after leader.

WALKING CREATES THE PATH

Even in her early dreams, Narcisa could not have envisioned how her life of leadership would come to be. People often want to see the way forward before they commit, but it just doesn't work that way. When I committed to ending world hunger, I had absolutely no idea how to do it. When I committed to preserving the world's tropical rainforests, I had no clue how that would happen. For those of us who are committed to ending racism in the United States, there is no road map. You can't figure it all out in advance and then do it.

As the W. S. Murray quote at the beginning of this book says, "The moment one definitely commits oneself, then Providence moves too." Things start to organize themselves around what needs to happen. It's not that obstacles, doubts, and worries go away, but you find your way through them. It's almost like a path opens up in the forest and you can then see the way forward—but not until you commit.

People often want to keep their options open; they fear being trapped. But in my experience, it is not making a commitment that traps you. Keeping your options open gets really tiresome and burdensome after a while. When you make your commitment and declare, "This is it!" then you have real freedom. I think of my 50-plus years of marriage to Bill Twist. In our early years, I was always worried that Bill was such a brilliant and handsome man, someone was going to take him away from me. Then, at a weeklong workshop, Bill and I realized that no matter what happened, we were life partners. We said, "This is our lifetime together, and we're not going anywhere." Once we were clear about our unconditional commitment, we knew we could handle anything together. When you are unshakable in your commitment, it frees you. It's so liberating!

Commitment is more powerful than anything. I don't really understand it, actually, but I see over and over again how it creates miracles for the world and for the person who is brave enough to make the commitment.

CHAPTER 2

Guidance from Source

*The most important decision we make is whether we believe
we live in a friendly or hostile universe.*
—ALBERT EINSTEIN

This quote is attributed to Einstein, a scientist who had a
deep spiritual life. It is said that Einstein felt the answer
to this fundamental question would determine how a person
lived. In an unfriendly universe, people would seek safety by
building walls; in a friendly universe, people would seek power
and safety by understanding the motives and workings of the
intelligence that put the stars in motion. If we see the universe
as neither friendly nor hostile, then we inhabit a random world
with no purpose or meaning. Einstein is not preaching, but
simply asking us to consider the context we live in—what we
choose to believe. Obviously, a friendly universe is an opening
to a different way of knowing that will impact how you live your
commitment.

My committed life had its roots in my growing-up years, and it derived from a connection to what I call Source. One could call it God, Spirit, a Higher Power or Purpose, the Tao, the Universe, Love, or simply intuition—any number of terms for the unseen forces that can inspire our lives. What is the source we choose to pay attention to? When we are committed to delivering on something that is way beyond what we can do on our own, ego takes a back seat. The commitment draws to you the messages, wisdom, and resources to fulfill itself, and you find yourself becoming an instrument of something larger than yourself.

Guidance can come from many sources or channels. Inner guidance comes through feelings in our own body—our heart, our guts, our intuition. It also comes through Nature, through teachers, through peak experiences, even through breakdowns and tragedies. If you are looking for it and paying attention, it will find you. In a way, the source is the listening. If you are uncomfortable with Spirit or spirituality, please know that you don't have to be spiritual to connect with Source. It can be called Integrity or Morality or Justice. You don't have to be guided by God; atheists can be just as committed, powerful, and effective coming from what they know to be true.

I am a spiritual person, and I believe an inspiring commitment is a call from the spirit of life itself. Being guided by Source is being in communion with what life wants to happen—what is yearning to be born or created or expressed. It is guidance from within, but in a way, it is impersonal: it comes through who is available. If you are called by Source or Spirit, it's not that you are better than someone else; being guided is not an ego thing you get credit for. There's a saying that goes something like, "Spirit doesn't care who flies, it just wants there to be flying."

I see now that it was Source that called to me, but it took me decades to understand how my access to Source laid the groundwork for my life of commitment.

MY CALL FROM SOURCE

I was born into privilege, the youngest of three daughters born to my mother, a civic leader, and my father, a well-known big band leader. Our brother was born when I was nine, and our grandmother lived with us as well. Our home in Evanston, Illinois, outside Chicago, was magnificent and filled with music and musicians. My dad's band, the Griff Williams Orchestra, traveled throughout the country. Life with my dad and "the boys in the band," as we called them, was super-fun. They were over at our house from time to time, including the "girl singers," who at one time included the likes of Dinah Shore. It was the 1950s, and everybody danced then. The United States had won the war, our economy was booming, and it seemed like everyone I knew was happy, especially our family.

In the summertime we kids got to go along when the band played resorts and state fairs with huge outdoor dance floors in the Midwest, the Poconos, and down South. In the winter the band played big hotels in New York, Chicago, Denver, and San Francisco, and my sisters and I explored the hidden realms behind the scenes. We could find our way through any hotel in America. It was such a blast!

I was a completely happy kid who took every kind of lesson possible—piano, voice, ballet, tap. I was an all-A student, popular, president of everything at school, and always the teacher's pet. My father traveled a lot, but when he was home, we played piano together. My childhood was oriented around pleasing my handsome, charismatic father, whom I adored.

And then he died. He had a heart attack in the middle of the night, and my mother found him on the morning of my 14th birthday. He was just 50 years old. My fairy-tale life disintegrated. The world as I knew it was over. I became absolutely despondent—in the depths of despair—and felt I had no one to turn to. My mother could barely function after his death. Here she was with four children and also feeling responsible for the band members and their families, as well as dealing with a lot of media attention. She was just totally shocked and overwhelmed and didn't have much space for us kids.

I was left to deal with my grief with my Sunday school teacher Sister Benjamin, a nun who was my refuge, my loving sanctuary. I don't know what I would have done without her. I was Catholic, and after my dad died, I became very religious and started going to Mass every day. I went to confession, I prayed the rosary, I prayed to the Blessed Mother. I even contemplated becoming a nun. Every morning I got up early enough to ride my bike to 5:30 or 6:00 a.m. Mass and then get back in time for my carpool to school. My friends had no idea I was doing this. I also regularly spent time at Cabrini Retreat Center in Des Plaines, near Evanston. It was a convent with small rooms containing just a bed, chair, and table, and there were beautiful gardens you could walk through. I went to Cabrini to pray. Now I would call it meditation, but then I prayed to God and Jesus and Mother Mary.

A month or two after my dad died, I had what I now call a mystical experience at Cabrini Retreat Center. I was in the garden praying in front of a statue of Blessed Mother Mary, and it seemed like she was looking right at me. I started to cry, and then I saw tears streaming down her face as well. As we were both weeping, she raised her arms up toward the sky, and I did the same. I was sobbing with joy and ecstasy. I didn't tell anyone because I almost couldn't believe it was true. Yet this part of my discovery of the realm of spirituality was crucial to healing my broken heart.

I had another experience a year or so later, again in those same gardens. My dad appeared and spoke to me, saying, "It's okay. You can play again. You can play the piano again." And after that, I was again able to embrace music in my life.

I had stopped playing piano and had become so religious because I thought my father's death was my fault. It's a convoluted story involving my piano teacher, Mrs. Block, who my dad hired to teach me every Tuesday morning at 7:30 a.m. A stout older woman with white hair and thick glasses, Mrs. Block was strict about practicing and gave me assignments each week that she kept track of in a notebook in pencil. She would write down, "Number 1, Mozart. Page 6 and 7," or "Hanon. Page 4 and 5. D Minor Scale."

At this time I was popular and just wanted to hang out with my friends. I did not want to practice piano, so I found a way to forge my assignments. I wrote in the notebook in her handwriting so that it looked as if the assignment were the same as the week before. I got away with playing the same thing week after week, and she would praise me: "That was excellent. You've been doing good work on your practicing. I'll tell your dad." Somehow, I never got caught. And I got really good at Mozart and Hanon!

And then my father died. Though I wasn't conscious of it at the time, I made up the story that cheating on my piano teacher was the same as cheating on my father, lying to my father, and that my lying had caused my father's death. I needed God to forgive me. I had to be so good to make up for my sin. I had to be perfect. I was going to be so good that my father in heaven would be proud of me. It did not become conscious for me that I blamed myself for my father's death until decades later.

At that time, I led a sort of double life: In eighth grade, when my friends were reading Nancy Drew mysteries and wondering when their breasts would grow and periods would start, I was secretly attending Mass every morning. Later, at Evanston Township High School, where there were about 4,000 students, I was president of my division, which had about 1,000 kids. I got excellent grades and was in honors everything. I was homecoming queen and went out with the captain of the football team. But there were times I wanted to go on retreat at Cabrini Center instead of going to a football game, and I would lie to my boyfriend and girlfriends and say I was going to visit my grandmother.

It was my father's death that catapulted me into a spiritual depth that I hadn't known before. Now I call it spiritual, but at the time, it was religious. I found a depth in myself, an inner life that almost no one knew about. It was like a parallel life I was living where I would pray, where I discovered silence and contemplation and soul—something amazing. I didn't tell my mom about any of this; she was already overwhelmed, and I feared it would add to her worries. I didn't tell my friends because they would have thought I was weird. When I wasn't studying and socializing, I found myself dwelling in this spiritual place, my own personal relationship with God.

In retrospect I can see how my father's death was both a huge heartbreak and a huge blessing in my life. With the passing of my father, it became clear to me that my life was a gift, and I was called by my earthly and heavenly fathers to make a difference with my life. In my grief, I had discovered the vastness of the inner life, what I now see as my access to and communion with Source, which still nourishes me. In that way, my dad led me to living a committed life.

MOTHER TERESA'S
LESSONS FOR ME

Stories of the ways in which Source has guided me since then could fill a book—and I have shared many of them in *The Soul of Money*. Worth repeating here is the story of my relationship with Mother Teresa, now Saint Teresa of Calcutta. She received the Nobel Peace Prize and is still one of the most admired beings on earth. As a Catholic, I had deep admiration for this tiny yet powerful woman who had founded the Missionaries of Charity, a congregation of more than 4,500 nuns working primarily in India but also in more than 100 other countries. As well as vows of chastity, poverty, and obedience, the Missionaries professed a fourth vow: to give "wholehearted free service to the poorest of the poor," which involved managing homes for sick and dying people as well as orphanages, schools, soup kitchens, clinics, and counseling programs.

My work with The Hunger Project had taken me to India several times, beginning in 1983, but it was not until 1991 that my long dream of being with Mother Teresa came true. A friend arranged a meeting at the orphanage in Old Delhi. As I stepped to the door, I reached down to pick up what I thought was a discarded newspaper and was shocked to find that it held a small newborn baby girl, the tiniest human being I had ever seen.

I carried the precious being into the orphanage and handed her to one of the nuns. The nuns immediately put me to work washing, feeding, and caring for the 50 or so children under two. I was enthralled with this blessed work, losing track of time until someone told me, "Mother Teresa will see you now."

Smiling and radiant, Mother Teresa grasped my head and hands in her gnarly hands and led me to a table and chairs to talk. Through tears I could not seem to stop from flowing, I told her of my commitment to the work of ending world hunger. She knew of my fundraising focus and acknowledged me warmly for the courage it took. She called herself "God's pencil" and bestowed that description on me as well. In the huge presence of this tiny person, I felt an unconditional love and connectedness to the universe that had me vibrating—until our intimate conversation was interrupted by the noisy appearance of two very large, very richly dressed Indians.

Apparently, this couple, dressed in opulent clothes and covered in gold and jewels, had been there previously and crashed into our conversation because, as the woman interrupted, "We didn't get a picture. We need to have a picture!" Without any greeting to either of us, the woman abruptly handed me her camera and then positioned Mother Teresa between them. She fussed a bit and tried to get Mother Teresa to look up at her, even rudely grabbing her chin and forcing it up. Shocked and horrified, I took the pictures, and the couple left without so much as a thank-you. While I seethed in anger at the intrusion, Mother Teresa carried on with me as if nothing had happened—though I could barely hear her through my upset. We parted, embracing each other, and I cried. Departing, I got in my taxi still fully enraged.

Over the next several hours I had a searing revelation about what had just happened. In the presence of one of the most inspiring human beings on the planet, I had been reduced to hatred and prejudice. While Mother Teresa could see this couple as children of God, deserving of the same kind of love and respect that she gave to the orphans in her care, I had judged them as rude, overbearing, and ugly, unworthy of inclusion in my circle of love. When I realized that I had to confront my own prejudice and lack of compassion, I felt great shame. I lit a candle and wrote Mother Teresa a letter asking for both her forgiveness and her counsel.

She responded a few weeks later in a handwritten letter admonishing me that while I felt it easy to feel compassion for people living in circumstances of hunger and poverty, I had not yet embraced the entitled, the wealthy, and the powerful—people who actually needed compassion as much as anyone on earth. She could see Christ in everyone, and I could not. "You must expand your circle of compassion to include the rich and powerful. Open your heart to them. . . . Do not shut them out. They are also your work."

It was then that I entered a new level of understanding about what I have come to call "the vicious cycle of wealth" that traps people in a prison of privilege. Although their material comforts are many, they are often deprived of emotional and spiritual comfort, and their wealth is no protection from human suffering. On the day I received Mother Teresa's letter, I made a commitment to open my heart to the rich and powerful with the same compassion I felt for people living with poverty and hunger. This simple vow transformed my ability to be a global fundraiser. I engaged with people at a soul level, enabling them to align their money with their deepest desires and commitments. From this paradigm, profound and lasting transformation could occur—in people's lives and in the world.

What brought me to Mother Teresa's orphanage on that particular day at the time of that wealthy couple's visit? I believe it was a gift from Source that launched me in my life's work of understanding and communicating universal truths about money and life. My relationship with a woman who so profoundly channeled a connection with the divine continued to offer me gifts—which are shared here in following chapters.

MY SPIRITUAL TEACHERS

Since my heart-opening relationship with Mother Teresa, I have had a number of spiritual teachers, some of whom would not call themselves spiritual but who had that impact on my being. Some you will hear about in this book. Two men in particular appear occasionally, so I want to introduce them properly here. Manari Ushigua is a shaman and leader of the Sápara people in Ecuador, and Arkan Lushwala is a ceremonial leader from Peru who is also from the Lakota tradition. Both men are highly educated in the Western world tradition, as well as in their own intensive training as shamans. Both have given me access not only to ancient teachings, but also to a deep and profound relationship with the natural world that has transformed how I experience the reality of life.

Manari, who has traveled the world speaking at conferences, meeting with some of the world's most powerful leaders in the United States and Europe, seems most at home walking barefoot and bare-chested with his machete in his home territory in the Amazon rainforest. One such walk with him years ago changed my life forever. I trailed behind him in my boots and jungle clothes as he cut a path through the forest. Suddenly he stopped and was silent, listening. He turned to me and said, "Can you feel them?"

I looked at him in confusion. "What do you mean?"

"Stop. Listen. Do you feel them?" A long pause. "The millions and millions of souls." And then I did feel them. My heart opened, and all the cells in my body seemed to connect with the souls of the trees, the vines, the mushrooms, the birds, the insects, all the millions of life forms that surrounded us. I had a vivid, bodily sense of the living world I inhabit, and that feeling has never left me.

Arkan Lushwala is a translator-interpreter between the Western world and ancient wisdom, offering traditional stories, teachings, and ceremonies that illuminate spiritual sources and experiences. One such occasion for me was a recent sunrise ceremony in the hills of Northern California, when he told our group that there was new power available to humanity from the sun. As he spoke and as the first rays of light struck my body, I felt the immense power of the sun to nourish life—all life, and my own life. Ever since, I have felt that I have access to that divine light—that I can tap into that source of nourishment in times of challenge. What a gift!

Many spiritual mentors have graced my life, some of whom are gone now: Frances Vaughan, Angeles Arrien, Wink Franklin, and Willis Harman—all of whom I connected with through the Institute of Noetic Sciences and the Fetzer Institute. They were great cutting-edge thinkers who mentored me, and I was blessed to be in the flow of their embodied wisdom for many years. I still feel their presence in my life.

It must be said, however, that spiritual teachers do not always live exemplary lives. They are human, after all. Even Mother

Teresa had her dark night of the soul, and some have blind spots and foibles that have caused them to lead themselves and their followers astray. While appreciating their teachings, I try not to put them on a pedestal but remain grateful for the openings they provide to a world beyond my ken.

My relationship with the Indigenous people of the Amazon rainforest has connected me with another great source of wisdom: plant medicine—in particular, the sacred ayahuasca plant, which they call *natem*. For thousands of years, the people of the forest have received guidance from the natural world in ayahuasca ceremonies conducted by shamans. In the trustworthy setting of the rainforest, guided by skilled shamans, I have on many occasions throughout the years experienced the transformational power of this medicine in my own life and have witnessed many other people having profound breakthroughs as a result of these sacred ceremonies.

RELYING ON FAITH

Whether you call it Providence or Source or God or just good luck, guidance from something other than our own limited thinking is available if we embrace it. If you cannot relate to the words *spiritual* or *faith*, you can think of it as guidance from an inner knowing or some larger force, like Nature or the Universe. Someone whose work has profoundly impacted me is author and teacher Will Keepin, who created what he calls the "Twelve Principles of Spiritual Leadership," presented at Schumacher College in England in 2013. In deepening our understanding of Source, I offer you his description of the eleventh principle:

The eleventh principle is to rely on faith. This is not some Pollyannaish naiveté, as many "realists" would interpret it. Rather it entails cultivating a deep trust in the unknown, recognizing the presence of "higher" or "divine" forces at work that we can trust completely without knowing their precise agendas or workings. It means invoking something beyond the traditional scientific worldview. It implies that there are invisible forces that we can draw upon and engage, firstly by knowing they are there; secondly, by asking or yearning for them to support us—or more precisely, asking them to allow us to serve on their behalf. Faith is understood not as blind adherence to any set of beliefs, but as a knowing from experience and intuition about intrinsic universal principles beyond our direct observation, and relying upon these principles, whatever they are, to support us in creating what we aspire to create. This actually brings great relief when we realize it really isn't up to us to figure out all the steps to manifest our unfolding vision, because we are participants in a larger cosmic will. Nevertheless, it is our job to discover what our unique gift is—our unique role—and for each person to give their gift as skillfully and generously as possible, while trusting that the rest will all work itself out.

However friendly you are with the notion of a "larger cosmic will," I encourage you to contemplate the Source or sources that you trust to guide you on your path of commitment.

CHAPTER 3

Answering the Call

I don't know Who—or what—put the question, I don't know when it was put. I don't even remember answering. But at some moment I did answer Yes to Someone—or Something—and from that hour I was certain that existence is meaningful and that, therefore, my life, in self-surrender, had a goal.

—DAG HAMMARSKJÖLD

We often don't know when or why we are called to do what is ours to do. Sometimes we are actively searching, and sometimes the inspiration just hits us over the head. Sometimes a commitment evolves slowly, surprising us as it reveals itself. I consider that I have (so far!) five major commitments in my life: ending world hunger, preserving the Amazon rainforest, changing the dream of the modern world, transforming how people relate to money, and empowering women to take their rightful place in what I call the Sophia Century. Each of these commitments was a response to a call from a Source—a yes to a Something—something beyond myself.

As the story in my introduction reveals, the commitment to ending hunger just took me over—completely out of the blue—around my 32nd birthday. Until that time, I had been a wife and mother living what many would consider a perfect life. The decade leading up to my taking a stand for ending hunger had been enviable, full of the bounty of the material world.

In 1963, I graduated from high school having been an honors student and president of my division, but I could still hardly believe that I had been accepted to Stanford University, where my father had attended.

At Stanford, my parallel lives of being a popular coed and a spiritual seeker continued. I was a pom-pom girl going out with the coolest fraternity guys and had a rich social and dating life. But I was also steeped in poetry, reading all sorts of poets both secular and mystical. I loved Rilke, e. e. cummings, Rabindranath Tagore, and Rumi. Poetry became almost like a new religion for me, very different from my Catholic experience of worship and prayer, sin and guilt. Poetry was about God; but it wasn't about church or rules, it was about the meaning of life. It wasn't about sin; it wasn't about being wrong or right. Poetry was about the soul. That was what I really loved about poetry. I began writing my own poems and even won the Stanford poetry contest.

In high school I hadn't paid much attention to the outside world; life was just about my boyfriend at the time and homecoming and getting into Stanford. My inner life was very much my own private world. But when President Kennedy was assassinated during my freshman year of college, it was a turning point for me. As the year progressed, I started paying attention to what was happening in the wider world, especially the harrowing developments of the Civil Rights Movement. By my junior year, I had gotten engaged with civil rights and other issues—especially stopping the Vietnam War, which was igniting protests on campuses all over the country. A social consciousness was arising in me, but I was on the fringes of activism, especially when I connected with the love of my life, Bill Twist, who would become my husband and full-on partner for more than 50 years. I introduce Bill here because he has been so inextricably engaged in my committed life.

CONNECTING WITH
THE LOVE OF MY LIFE

At Stanford, Bill was a BMOC (big man on campus)—tall and impossibly handsome with blond hair, blue eyes, and a killer physique. He came from a privileged family in Newport Beach that was all about sailing and the yacht club. He was studying engineering and was a great athlete—a champion sailor on the sailing team as well as playing on the tennis team and the basketball team. Brilliant and charming, he was also a bit of a rascal. A fraternity prank at the beginning of his senior year got him kicked out of school, and he spent a year sailing in the South Seas, joining and getting out of the Marine Corps, and working part-time at an engineering firm.

When he returned to Stanford in January 1966, we had a falling-off-a-cliff kind of romance. I fell madly in love with him, and he fell madly in love with me. He was so confident and fun, completely at home in his own skin. I thought he was the healthiest person I'd ever met. We spent every waking minute together. On New Year's Eve eve, December 30, 1966, we were married in a red-and-white-themed ceremony in Chicago. My father's orchestra came back together for the first time since his death in 1959. They played, we danced, and I felt like the luckiest woman in the world.

Bill and I graduated from Stanford in June 1967, and the next few years seemed like a perfect trajectory toward a perfect life: He went to business school at Northwestern University in Chicago, and I was the breadwinner, teaching first grade, and then drama, dance, and music, at Sacred Heart School. In 1969, our son Basil was born, right when Bill was graduating. He was at the top of his class and had an array of great job offers, so we were able to fulfill our dream of moving to San Francisco. His first salary was maybe $90,000 or $100,000, which felt to me like a zillion dollars.

We took a small apartment on Russian Hill that had 127 steps from the street to our third-floor door. It was a real pain to negotiate a baby, his paraphernalia, and groceries up those stairs, but once there, the panoramic view of the city and the San Francisco Bay made up for it. You felt free. You could think big. But all I could think about was being a mother. Being Catholic, I had baby number two, Summer, in 1971, and baby number three, Zachary, in 1973. So I was all about these three little kids and logistics and the groceries while Bill became a rising star in the business world. We did move to a more practical apartment, and I taught school again, as well as drama, music, and dance, and I got involved in a puppet workshop, making puppets and performing at hospitals and old folks' homes. But mostly I aimed to be the perfect wife, worrying about my weight, my looks, my clothes, and "keeping up with the Joneses."

THE SIREN SONG OF MONEY

By 1973, Bill was really making money. He worked at Itel Corporation with a bunch of his friends who were Stanford or Harvard and Northwestern MBAs. With the money flowing, what I have called "the siren song of success" was calling us. It seemed I had everything anyone could want from life, but it was not as ideal as it might have seemed.

As I described in *The Soul of Money*, we inhabited a world of affluence where the money was plentiful, and we kept spending more and more. This lifestyle took its toll on our family life, as Bill worked long hours and traveled, and I struggled with the constant upgrades needed to match our friends' lifestyles. I was engrossed in living a full-on yuppie life with the appropriately splendid house, the BMW, the designer clothes, the fine wines and luxurious vacations. The kids were well-cared-for by a nanny and babysitters, but they were not the focus of our lives that we had intended. I wasn't conscious that anything was missing in my beautiful life, but something deep inside must have been whispering to me. Under this enviable surface, I was often anxious and miserable. I was constantly doubting myself, comparing myself with other women, feeling inadequate, and worrying that Bill would leave me.

One night we were at a party in Sausalito, and I saw my friend Sandra, who was looking particularly good. I said so, and she told me, "Yeah, I lost 15 pounds. I feel really great. But you know what really happened? I took this course called est. It was just the most amazing experience. Two weekends, one leader, and 250 people in a hotel ballroom. You cannot believe what happened to me. The whole world's a different place for me. I feel so alive, so excited about life."

I said, "Wow! Where do I sign? I want to do it." Thus began a complete transformation in my life. With the est Training, I entered a world I had never even imagined.

ENTERING THE WORLD OF EST

If you were a culturally aware person during the 1970s and 1980s, you probably know about Werner Erhard and the est Training. And if you've taken the training yourself, you will have more of a sense of my experience. If not, you may recall that it was criticized as a cult and lampooned as a self-help boondoggle. But for many thousands of people in the United States and internationally, it was a life-altering experience, and for me it became a primary source of my lifetime of commitment.

It was in the est Training that I had the searing recognition that I had blamed myself for my father's death—that cheating on my piano lessons and lying to him about it had somehow contributed to his dying—and I began the process of forgiving myself. Also important to me was discovering that in my current life I was always struggling to be something, someone, that I wasn't. I wanted to be as smart as Sandra, to be as beautiful as Jerri, and to have a house like Libby's. Despite all I had, inside I felt insufficient and insecure. The est Training transformed that—and so much more. I discovered who I was. I took responsibility for my life in a new way and saw it as a gift to be given to the world.

I came home from the experience elated, inspired, and in love with life. I persuaded Bill and all our friends to take the training, and I began volunteering—assisting, it was called—at a host of est trainings and guest seminars. I began leading the seminars myself and became a major player in the San Francisco est Center. Soon I was in the role of managing Sphere of Influence People (SOIPs—what we called the VIPs). These were folks who were famous and were interested in taking the est Training but didn't want people to know about it. I was in charge of creating a special confidential training for them. It was through this work that I came in personal contact with the great inventor and visionary, R. Buckminster Fuller. For Bucky, as he was known, everything began with a personal commitment, the kind of personal responsibility that was at the heart of the est Training.

After hearing Bucky speak at the Integrity Day event that I described in chapter 1, I was certain that if Buckminster Fuller met Werner Erhard, a miracle would occur. Some months later, my est colleague Ronn Landsman and I came across an SOIP application from Jamie Snyder, who mentioned that he was the grandson of Buckminster Fuller. We were thrilled that we now had a connection to the great man. Through Jamie, we managed to engineer a meeting of Bucky and Werner in January 1977, when Bucky was in San Francisco. The meeting was supposed to be a couple of hours, but at the end of that time, both men canceled whatever had been subsequently scheduled in order that they could continue talking. That initial meeting turned into three or four days of constant conversation between the two men and produced a historic collaboration that became the foundation for the creation of The Hunger Project.

THE BEGINNING OF
THE HUNGER PROJECT

The question that Bucky and Werner addressed together was, "What is the most fundamental breakdown in the human family?" At that time, there were 4.3 billion people on Earth, and a billion people—a quarter of humanity—were hungry all of the time. Fifteen million people each year died of starvation and malnutrition, most of them children under the age of five. The two men were clear that chronic hunger and malnutrition was not an issue of food—the world produced enough food for everyone—but an issue of the integrity of humanity. People not being able to feed themselves or their children was humanity's most fundamental failure, an indictment of our lack of commitment to the human family.

It was out of these conversations that Werner Erhard made his own personal commitment to initiate a project to end world hunger by the end of the century. In collaboration with Bucky; singer John Denver; Robert Fuller, president of Oberlin College; and others, he realized that what was missing was not solutions for hunger, but rather the commitment to end it. This new project would generate the worldwide commitment to make the end of hunger "an idea whose time has come," and it would do so by enrolling graduates of the est Training to commit themselves personally to this new context.

As I recounted earlier, there was a great deal of opposition to this project from the est Advisory Board, but eventually they came around, and in fall 1977, I became part of the team that was launching events in 11 US cities with tens of thousands of est graduates attending. Werner's request of his audiences was that they make a personal commitment to the end of hunger. The vehicle for taking this stand was a simple enrollment card that said, "The Hunger Project is mine completely. I am willing to be responsible for making the end of hunger and starvation an idea whose time has come." The card offered several ways of participating, such as fasting, contributing money, or enrolling others.

Once launched, The Hunger Project certainly had its detractors. "You can't eat words" summed up the misunderstanding of Werner's strategy that appeared in the media. A hunger organization that focused on harnessing commitment was a radical departure from the food aid and development strategies that had to date been employed by the hunger-response community. And of course, there were those who claimed it was not possible to achieve such a goal in 20 years, if at all, believing human hunger and starvation to be "just the way it is" on planet Earth.

PERSONALLY COMMITTING
TO THE END OF HUNGER

In the decades since, eradicating extreme poverty and hunger became a global goal, moving to the top of the United Nations Sustainable Development Goals for 2030. This was all unthinkable in 1977, but the individual, personal commitment of millions of people had created the collective will and the political possibility for a world free from hunger. For the past four decades, The Hunger Project has played a powerful role in galvanizing a constituency for the end of hunger and in implementing strategies aimed at empowering hungry people to feed themselves. But in those first few years, The Hunger Project was focused on enrollment, education, and communication. With many thousands of est graduates gathering signatures on enrollment cards, the number of people making that commitment grew to six million worldwide within just a few years. And this was before computers and the Internet! It was personal contact—at events, at tables outside grocery stores, in offices and schools—that brought the possibility of a world free from hunger into the hearts and minds of millions of people throughout the world. And it was personal commitment that motivated people and fueled a movement that now has the end of hunger in its sights.

So what did signing a card have to do with ending world hunger? Millions of people signed that card and then probably never thought about it again. But there were perhaps millions more who, in the years that followed, found themselves paying attention to the news about hunger, being caught up in events like Live Aid, and perhaps contributing money not just to food aid in famines but to an array of development organizations. And I know that there were many thousands who, like me, began to live that commitment in their daily lives. We became the commitment; we reorganized our lives and recalibrated our choices, relationships, and finances to reflect our stand. We became a connected core of people who answered the call to source this new and powerful commitment of the human family, and I became one of the leaders of that movement.

For two decades, The Hunger Project was my life, and I assumed that would be the case until hunger was ended or until I died; I hoped the former would come first! I could not have imagined that another call, totally unexpected and disruptive, would launch me on a magical mystery tour into a new direction for my committed life.

A MYSTERIOUS INVITATION UPENDS MY LIFE

In 1994, I was thoroughly engaged in my organizing and fund-raising work with The Hunger Project, traveling to Europe, Asia, and Africa, when I accepted an invitation to a gathering in Guatemala. Our Hunger Project work did not take me to Central and South America, but I went at the invitation of a friend and Hunger Project donor to work with his nonprofit's board of directors. Included in the group was John Perkins, a man I greatly admired, who had become an economic development consultant but had roots as a Peace Corps volunteer in the Ecuadorean Amazon, where he had trained as a shaman.

Through John's connection to a local Mayan shaman, Roberto Poz, our group gathered outside at midnight for a ceremony. It was my first-ever shamanic ceremony, and it did not include any mind-altering substances. Our group of 12 was asked to lie down with our feet toward the fire and instructed to "journey." I had no idea what that meant, but I closed my eyes and became mesmerized by John's quiet drumming and Roberto's hypnotic chanting. Soon, I was no longer inhabiting my body. I became a bird with gigantic wings and a great beak, and I began to fly far up into the brilliant, starry night, still hearing the chanting and drumming. As the light of dawn appeared, I could see that I was flying over a vast, unending forest of green, pristine and magnificent. My vision was so acute, I could see through the canopy to the forest floor, to the creatures below, and it was exhilarating.

Then the forest yielded a mystifying vision: floating up toward me through the canopy were the disembodied faces of men with orange geometric shapes painted on them, and yellow, red, and black feather crowns on their heads. They spoke to me in a language I did not understand, calling to me in a poignant and plaintive tone. They floated away and reappeared several times—hypnotic and beautiful—until a loud drumbeat called me back, and I was once more a human being in a circle of tired and disoriented people. The shaman asked us each to share our experience, and almost everyone recounted becoming an animal of some kind.

When I described my flight as a bird over the forest and the encounter with the men with face paint and headdresses, the shaman, through John, told me that mine was not a normal vision, but a communication that I must respond to. "People somewhere are calling to you, and you must go to them."

I had no idea what to do next, but John knew exactly who those calling were and where they were. He recognized the facial markings and the feather headdresses. He said, "Lynne, it's the Achuar people deep in the Amazon rainforest. I was just there with a neighboring tribe, the Shuar people, and there was an Achuar warring party that entered our camp. They told us that they are ready for contact with the outside world, and they are wisely calling for it. They have been told in their dreams and ceremonies that they need to partner with people who can support them in preserving their land and culture. This is an extraordinary opportunity, and you and I have to respond and go there."

I said, "John, no way. I don't know anything about the Amazon. I don't speak Spanish. I'm just here for this one week. That's your work—you go. I need to go to Africa." And that's what I proceeded to do, even though John warned me that the visions would not stop until I answered them.

Soon I was in Accra, Ghana, for a board meeting for The Hunger Project of Ghana, sitting around a table with a team of Ghanaians, five men and three women. As we sat around a table in conversation, I started to see orange geometric face paint appear on the faces of the men. Not the women, just the men. No one else saw anything. I was so shaken by the visions that I burst into tears and ended up leaving the meeting and Ghana as soon as possible, saying I was sick and needed to get home. But even on the long airplane journey, from Accra to Frankfurt to New York to San Francisco, I continued to see the painted faces and feather crowns—appearing every hour or so, whether my eyes were open or shut.

Once home, I was freaked out, of course—exhausted, confused, and discombobulated. I thought I was going crazy. I tried to rest, but the faces did not stop, when I was waking, sleeping, even driving. I knew that this was not right, that this could not continue, so I began to try to contact John Perkins, who I found out was still in the Amazon. It seemed like months, but it was probably only a few days, before he got back to me. "Yes, Lynne," he said, "the faces are real. It is a communication from the Achuar. They're asking for contact from the outside world. They want us to come to them with 12 people who have open hearts, people who have global voice that can be heard in some way around the world, people who know the rainforest is critical to the future of life, and people who will respect the ways of the shaman, and who are open to our wisdom."

I knew then that I had to go. What I did not know or even suspect was that this journey would shift the focus of my life and begin a remarkable adventure into a world and a culture that would shape my future and launch a worldwide movement as well. It's a story that I will recount more fully throughout this book, but for now, I offer it simply as an example of a calling—which I consider to be not just a call from the Achuar, but a call from the rainforest, a call from life itself and from the future we have yet to create.

THE "SOUL" OF MONEY

Some years after the call from the rainforest that launched the Pachamama Alliance, another calling stirred me: to illuminate for people what I came to call the "soul" of money. Does money have a soul? Maybe not, but we do. And we can use money in a way that's consistent with the depth and longings of our soul. When we approach our relationship with money consciously and begin to examine our attitudes toward how we earn it, spend it, invest it, and give it away, money can be an expression of who we are rather than something that we use to acquire more stuff or fill the emptiness inside.

In my years as a fundraiser for The Hunger Project, raising hundreds of millions of dollars, I gained a unique perspective on how dysfunctional money is in people's lives—whether they are people of great wealth or people living with little or nothing. I recognized the differences between these two, but I also came to see the commonalities in how money dominates and stresses all of our lives. I also witnessed the immense healing power of money when it is used to express our highest ideals, values, and commitments. My insight into the debilitating effects of the toxic myth of scarcity and the miraculous power of living from a paradigm of sufficiency led me to write my first book, *The Soul of Money: Transforming Your Relationship with Money and Life.* The book's success led to opportunities for me to speak widely and offer training programs and coaching through the Soul of Money Institute.

EMPOWERING WOMEN IN
THE SOPHIA CENTURY

My stand for the empowerment of women evolved throughout all three of these previous commitments. I came of age when the women's movement was waking us to the imbalances and injustices of the patriarchy. I became a feminist, but it was not until I started working with The Hunger Project that I experienced the daunting challenges faced by women worldwide—not only the resource-poor, but females of all standing in almost every country of the world. I was further schooled in the marginalization of women by my involvement with the Nobel Women's Initiative. When this organization of eight women Nobel Peace Prize laureates first called on me to help with strategic planning and fundraising, I had no idea that I would be exposed to some of the most heart-wrenching suffering imaginable as they campaigned to stop violence and sexual abuse of women caught in war and conflicts.

My work with "the Nobels," as I call them, took me to some of the darkest places in the world, where I saw and heard things that stirred me at the deepest part of who I've known myself to be. It was sometimes hard to recover from the haunting and horrific tales of violence, but once I got into action, I began to feel helpful and therefore hopeful. Some stories about this experience will follow later in this book. For now, suffice it to say these courageous women showed me how desperately the world needs to embrace feminine values, ideals, and characteristics.

I speak now about our time—the 21st century—as the Sophia Century, the term *Sophia* referring to the wisdom of the feminine. The 20th century was dominated by war and the fear of war for 100 years. Now, at the beginning of the third millennium, is the time for the feminine to rise: for both women and men to find the full expression of their yin energy to balance the overbearing yang of the patriarchy.

This era is described by a beautiful prophecy about the 21st century from the Baha'i faith. The Baha'i faith says that the bird of humanity has two great wings—a male wing and a female wing—and that for centuries, these two wings have not been of equal strength. The male wing has been fully extended, fully expressed, while the female wing has been folded in, not fully extended, not fully expressed. In order for the bird to keep itself afloat, its male wing has become overdeveloped, overmuscular, even violent. Without its balancing counterpart, the bird of humanity has been continually flying in circles, unable to reach the heights of real attainment. The prophecy says that in the 21st century, the female wing of the bird of humanity will fully extend itself and be expressed in all of us. The male wing will then relax, and with two wings fully extended and of equivalent strength, the bird of humanity will soar to new heights.

If we are looking to transform our future, we need to uplift and enliven heart-centered feminine values—compassion, empathy, nurturance, diversity, equity, humility, and love. The Sophia Century calls to both women and men to bring balance and interdependence into the new world we are creating.

Indeed, it is Mother Earth herself who is issuing a call for a new alignment of the sexes. As humanity careens toward an uncertain future, we are in short supply of wisdom and the values that will ultimately bring us peace and healing. Our cascading crises—climate change; global pandemics; a reckoning with painful legacies of centuries of colonialism, racism, sexism, and white supremacy; the extinction of half the world's species; extreme economic inequality; the decline of civil discourse; and growing threats to our democracy—all have their roots in the separation and domination inherent in a patriarchal system. Our Mother is calling to us, in the strongest possible way, threatening even our survival in order to have us listen at last to the suppressed values of the feminine.

Perhaps you have heard a call—a still, small voice or a booming wake-up call. Perhaps life itself and your future are calling you as well. As you engage with this book, I invite you to open yourself to a message or a vision. You do not have to be a religious or spiritual person to be connected to something larger than yourself. Just ask, *What are the deepest values that generate my desire to serve?* As you contemplate your own purpose and commitment, what foundational experiences can guide and empower you?

CHAPTER 4

Taking a Stand

*Give me a lever and a place to stand and I will move
the earth.*

—ARCHIMEDES

I love this quote from the Greek mathematician Archimedes two millennia ago, because I believe that when we take a stand for something, we can move the world and change the course of history. Taking a stand comes from the deepest part of you—the very heart of who you are. Living your stand gives you clarity and power as well as the capacity to engage people and institutions to literally move the Earth. A stand is something that is uplifting and enhances life. It is usually for something rather than against something. You can be against police brutality, but what you stand for is justice for all.

A stand is visionary and focuses on the big picture. It's like a direction for the human journey. Usually a stand is something larger than you could possibly accomplish by yourself, even over a lifetime. You don't end up getting credit. However, when you take a stand, you have access to vision—you're in the flow of what wants to happen, and it uses your life. Your life is lit up with meaning and purpose and usefulness. It is not only what will make your life joyous and fulfilling; it is what is called for on the planet. We all are needed, every single one of us. Every single one of us is an important player in stepping up to the challenges of this century.

Taking a stand is what gives rise to making a commitment—something that you can—and aim to—accomplish. You could think of the words *purpose*, *stand*, and *commitment* as meaning the same thing, but I actually make a distinction. I have in mind a sort of flow: taking a stand leads to a commitment or commitments, which gives your life purpose. In other words, finding your purpose begins with a stand. Our stand is our vision, and our lever is our commitment.

My first stand was for the end of hunger and starvation on this planet. That stand led to my commitment to The Hunger Project and to my purpose of raising awareness and money for a global transformation. That stand led to others over the past few decades: preserving the Amazon rainforest for its inhabitants and for the world, changing the dream of the modern world away from separation toward interconnection, generating a new consciousness about money based on the context of sufficiency, and empowering women to take their rightful place as equal partners with men in order to bring the world into balance. These five commitments come together in the overarching stand of my life: creating a world that works for everyone with no one and nothing left out—what I call a *you and me* world.

TWO STANDS HALF A WORLD APART

In fulfilling my commitments, I have witnessed many, many transformations that have occurred when individuals and groups of people have taken a stand. Most memorable is the stand taken together by two groups of seven women half a world apart geographically and worlds apart in their lives.

In 1984 and 1985, there was an absolutely horrific famine in the Horn of Africa, primarily centered in Ethiopia, where millions of people were starving, and a million people actually starved to death in what's called the Rift Valley. This famine drew the attention of the world, thanks to a powerful BBC documentary and the involvement of music superstars who produced the Live Aid concert, which was broadcast internationally and raised $127 million for famine relief.

After that famine, The Hunger Project sent me to a place called Ifat Tibuga in the Rift Valley, where hundreds of thousands of people, mostly children, had had a terrible death. I found myself sitting around a dry well with seven women who had lost every single one of their children to starvation. Can you imagine? I can barely fathom losing one child: the oldest woman there had lost all of her eleven children. I engaged with these grieving mothers in a ritual consistent with the tradition of this area: they wanted to tell the story of the death of each child.

One by one in this circle, the women told in excruciating detail the story of each child's death, going from the oldest to the youngest. After each story, we would all grieve with the mother, wailing, screaming, and holding each other, and then she would tell us about the next one. They spoke their names, Mohammed, then Malika, then the baby that was nourished at her breast until there was no more milk because the mother had had no water in seven days. The little baby would stop sucking, and when she looked down, she had stopped breathing and was dead at her breast. It took five days and five nights to complete the circle. At the end of that, we were completely exhausted and spent—emotionally, physically, spiritually. It was a hugely cathartic experience for them, of course; and for me, it was just overwhelming.

Then, something miraculous happened. These were young women who, due to the tragedy, were destined to live the rest of their lives as childless mothers, a difficult fate in Ethiopia, but something had been born out of their shared grief. Somehow, they saw the possibility of regenerating their tragic lives and having them make a difference. Although none of them could read or write, they each made a commitment to get educated and to devote the rest of their lives to making sure that other mothers would not go through the hell they had endured. I was stunned by the stand they had taken. I had no idea how they might accomplish such a commitment, and I doubt they did either.

Within a few days of leaving Ethiopia, I found myself in another meeting with seven women, now in an elegant apartment on Fifth Avenue in New York City. This circle of women were the affluent, stylish wives of Wall Street magnates. I'm not sure what their husbands did, but they were making tons of money. These women had formed an investment club and wanted to talk about money and contribution. All I could manage to talk about was my recent experience in Ethiopia, sobbing the whole time. The women cried along with me, feeling the connection of motherhood and the deep tragedy of losing children. Then a possibility struck me: "There's seven of you and seven of them. Maybe you can find a way to do something together."

It was clear to me that these New York women were starving in a different way: they were starved for meaning in their lives.

They were rich in resources and talent and connections, but they were hungry to make a difference. The whole framework of rich and poor was turned on its head. There are no "haves" and "have-nots." You can't collapse people's finances into who they are, when in fact they are whole and complete people who have hurts, wounds, longings, and love. To define them or label them by their circumstances demeans and undermines who they are. Both of these groups of women had incredible assets. The New York women had huge amounts of money, education, and connections; the Ethiopian women had a different set of assets: knowledge—of people and the environment—as well as tremendous strength, courage, and resilience. They had a great deal to give to each other, and once that possibility was revealed, it was completely transformational.

The seven New York women also took a stand. They vowed that they would partner with the seven women in Ethiopia and offer them any assistance they could in living up to their stand of taking care of themselves and getting educated for service. They did not imagine then how the Ethiopian women would end up contributing to their lives as well, enabling them to draw on their strength and resilience as they struggled with divorce and challenges with their own children.

The New York women visited Ethiopia and created a collaboration that lasted many years, during which the Ethiopian women were able to get educated. Three got PhDs and ended up serving in government; one runs a huge scientific institute, and another, who became an attorney, runs the largest and most prolific law firm serving the rights of women in Ethiopia.

It was a divine experience for the New York women as well. Spurred by a deep sense of their humanity, they started organizations and foundations; they brought their children to Ethiopia and saw them shift from being haughty and entitled to being kind and compassionate human beings. All sorts of beautiful things happened when each of the groups could see and then take a stand for a new possibility for their lives.

I am sure that this international relationship had its problems and issues. When you take a stand and are committed, it doesn't mean you leave your ego behind and don't get upset or angry. You can still get caught up in upsets, but ultimately you relinquish all that in service of the stand you've taken.

TAKING A STAND
VERSUS A POSITION

Now, it is important to make a distinction that is crucial to living a committed life: understanding the difference between taking a stand and taking a position. They are not only not the same; they are in entirely different domains. As I've said, a stand is visionary, looking at the big picture. The positions we take have a smaller scope and usually reflect our beliefs and opinions. Taking a position, however right we may consider it to be, creates its opposition: "up" calls forth "down"; "left" sets up "right"; "us" brings forth "them"; "pro-choice" generates "pro-life." And the more entrenched you are in pro-life, the more entrenched the response will be in pro-choice. That is the nature of positionality. So while positions are important and useful, they can also get us into trouble—trapping us in ideology and conflict.

Another way of looking at a position is that it's a point of view, like a literal point—a place, like a geographic location, from which you see the world. If you are sitting in the back of an auditorium looking at the stage, you have a point of view of the speaker. If you're sitting on the side of the auditorium, maybe halfway up, you have a different point of view of the speaker. If you're standing backstage and you're looking from there, you see the back of the speaker. All three points of view are 100 percent accurate for the person who has them. But if you start identifying with your point of view, believing that it's right and any other point of view is wrong, and you try to get people to agree with your point of view, it's an exercise in futility because every point of view has its own validity.

An authentic stand can take into account all positions so that you have the capacity to see and even incorporate all points of view. When you take a stand, you release yourself from your position or any position. When you can relinquish your point of view and free yourself from it, what you end up with is vision. Vision is the capacity to see, and from a place of vision, you can see all points of view. It is as if you are 30,000 feet up, and looking down, you can see how valid and useful every point of view is—and how true it is for the person who is holding it.

So, points of view are not wrong; they are very important and useful. You just need to know that your position is not who you are and that you can "get off it"—literally move off your point of view. You can move from this chair to that chair. But, when people think they are their point of view, that's when we create ideologies that trap us.

If you are a visionary, you have the wherewithal and grace to get off your position. So, stand takers are able to drop down into the fray and take positions, but they only do that in a way that forwards the intent of their stand. And then you appreciate and can listen to and be informed by every position. You can hear it because you're not about refuting it, or arguing with it, or trying to decide whether or not it's right or wrong—you give that up. You allow the position to contribute.

VAN JONES AND
THE FIRST STEP ACT

One of the most inspiring examples of someone who does not let his positions get in the way of his stand is Van Jones. I have been privileged to call Van a friend and colleague for many years. Van is currently best known as a political commentator on CNN, but he has had a lifelong career as an activist on behalf of underrepresented people. To me, Van Jones is a visionary who represents the epitome of living a committed life. What is remarkable about Van is his ability to see all sides of an issue and to see the humanity in all people no matter what positions they hold. I'm sure that is why Jeff Bezos chose him as one of the first two recipients of his 2021 Courage and Civility Award, which came with a $100 million prize to be distributed as Van chooses.

Courage and civility were certainly on display when Van was one of the principal people trying to negotiate prison reform during the Trump administration. Overcriminalization and mass incarceration in America had begun to receive attention as more and more people became aware that the United States locked up more people than any other country in the world. Our 2.2 million prisoners in a population of 350 million is 1.2 million more than China's with a population of 1 billion. While both Democrats and Republicans had contributed to this situation, there were the stirrings of bipartisan support for prison reform, as conservatives were concerned about costs and conditions.

Van, who had become an influential political commentator on CNN, had founded an organization called #cut50 (now called Dream Corps JUSTICE), aimed at reducing the US prison population by 50 percent. He had the courage to reach across the aisle for support for reform from Trump's son-in-law,

Jared Kushner, whose father had served time in a federal prison, and found some alignment there. Kushner and others, including the Koch brothers, were supporting legislation called the First Step Act, aimed at making the federal prison system fairer, more humane, and more focused on rehabilitation. The First Step Act was not the sweeping reform that progressive Democrats wanted to see enacted, but it would bring early release to at least 20,000 people and improve conditions for tens of thousands more. At a time when the partisan divide was egregiously wide, Van and his team began an intensive campaign to get the bill passed—only to find that many progressive leaders and organizations were against what they considered to be weak legislation that did not go nearly far enough and if passed would give a boost to Donald Trump and the Republican Party.

Partisan positionality played a prominent role in the opposition to passing the act. As Van describes it, "People as wise and good as John Lewis aggressively opposed the bill. And so all of my heroes and mentors and she-roes, and colleagues in the movement, were united—a wall of opposition to what I was doing—just by me reaching across the aisle and shaking hands with Jared Kushner. But I saw it differently. My view was we should get people out of prison. The idea that I was not going to reach across a gap that small to free 20,000 people from the hell of federal prison when I had the opportunity to do so did not even occur to me. It didn't occur to me to walk away. And it was a roller-coaster ride."

This is where the distinction of stand versus position played out. Van took a stand for getting people out of prison. This was an opportunity to free thousands and improve conditions for tens of thousands as well as to take much-needed bipartisan action. It wasn't everything, but it was a beginning—a first step.

His most vocal opponents turned out to be progressives and his Black activist colleagues and friends who attacked him vociferously for "legitimizing" Kushner and Trump. He was called a dupe, a sellout, an Uncle Tom, and worse. He was shunned and vilified. Van says he was deeply wounded, but he knew that he could not let this moment pass. He would not let political positionality stand in the way of reforms that would not only free people but also build momentum for more comprehensive bipartisan legislation.

Due in large part to Van's tireless efforts, the First Step Act went on to pass by wide margins in both the House and the Senate, and Trump signed the bill, giving one of the signing pens to Van. And in the end, the bump in Black support for Trump did not happen. Van says, "The idea that I was a sellout and a fool—I didn't see that. Bobby Kennedy said moral courage is not standing up to your enemies; moral courage is standing up to your friends when they're wrong. And my friends were wrong to be willing to leave 2.2 million people behind bars with no hope, no help, no matter who's the president. Sometimes you have to take a stand for the right outcome, especially when you have that moment."

Van continues to be an extraordinary bridge-builder in the realms of politics and social justice. More than anyone I know, he is a stand for transforming our bitter differences into constructive action for real change. His most recent book is *Beyond the Messy Truth: How We Came Apart, How We Come Together*. He challenges us to stand in each other's shoes, to abandon the right/wrong dichotomy, and to come together to solve our toughest problems. One of my favorite video segments from the Pachamama Alliance's Awakening the Dreamer Symposium is Van talking about how taking a stand becomes a standing ovation:

I don't think an authentic stand comes from your head. I think an authentic stand comes from your heart. If your child is sick, right . . . something happens in you to make a miracle, to make a miracle. And if you start thinking about it, you'll sit down. But if you feel it, you'll stand up! That's the amazing thing about this—it's that when you stand up, you license other people to stand up. Now you standing up by yourself don't make a dad gum bit of difference—in the rational world. You're just one fool standing up. But have you ever seen a standing ovation? It starts with one fool standing up. And then pretty soon the whole stadium is standing up, and it's a different moment.

The capacity to take a stand and to live it is the core of a committed life, and it is available to everyone—everyone has the capacity to do that. If you were drawn to this book, you may be longing to unlock that in yourself, or maybe it is there already and you want to deepen it. Or maybe you didn't have a clue that something like that existed until now. Living a stand isn't easy; it takes enormous courage. You literally give up your identity and become the stand you've taken, but it is an experience of absolute and total freedom.

TAKING A STAND WITH YOUR MONEY

As a fundraiser and philanthropist myself, I believe that one place everyone can take a stand is with their money. You don't have to leave your job or revolutionize your business or live off the grid. The everyday choices you make about how you spend your money and what you support with it are powerful statements of your values and who you are. You can express your stand for the environment by living a low-carbon lifestyle and resisting the pressure to consume more. You can support social justice in your community by contributing to any number of community services like shelters and food banks. If you are an employer, you can invest in your employees' health and well-being with appropriate salaries and benefits. You can contribute to personal and spiritual fulfillment by deepening your own practices and looking out for friends and neighbors.

Whatever the nature of your own commitment and call to action, I invite you to take a stand for sufficiency and generosity by using your money to help create the world you want to see. No matter where you are in terms of wealth and disposable income, you can fund the causes you care about at the local, national, and global levels. Choose the organizations that best express your values and support them. Even small, regular donations make a huge difference, especially when compounded over time. I say if you can't be an activist, then fund one!

PART II

The Soul of Commitment

Discovering the distinctions of living a committed life gives you access to new ways of thinking and being that will empower you and serve the mission you seek to fulfill.

CHAPTER 5

Transformation

Again and again in history some people wake up. They have no ground in the crowd and move to broader deeper laws. They carry strange customs with them and demand room for bold and audacious action. The future speaks ruthlessly through them. They change the world.

—RAINER MARIA RILKE

While I was working with my editor on this book, he asked me, "What is your theory of change?" I had to think about that. After a while I responded that my life isn't about change; it's about transformation. I am seeking the kind of impact in the world that Rilke speaks of—where the future ruthlessly calls forth bold and audacious action. And so, I make a distinction between change and transformation.

Transformation is a complete and total shift in the nature and dynamics of what's happening. When you change a situation, sometimes it really is a game changer, but often what you're actually looking for is a transformation and you don't even know it. When you set out to make change in the world, you are responding and reacting to what currently exists; you aim to make it less, more, different, or better. Transformation, however, creates something anew. The clearest example is the extraordinary transformation of the caterpillar into a butterfly —two creatures whose forms could hardly be more different.

THE DIFFERENT DYNAMICS OF CHANGE AND TRANSFORMATION

To make change, you generally have to make something wrong or undesirable: "This is not right—we have to change it." A perfect example is our political process. In every election cycle, politicians run for office professing that things need to change. They point to what's not working, what's wrong, what's ineffective or off course. They insult it, criticize it, judge it to be undesirable and something that must not continue. And then they—sometimes—offer their alternative, their opposing idea or different future. Change is useful, and it's important. We need to be able to make changes in our lives—in our relationships, our diet, our decisions, and our political leaders. When you change a situation, the circumstances may get moved around and different outcomes may result, but unless there is a fundamental shift in how the situation is perceived, the same problems may arise again and again. I think of the quote attributed to Einstein: "We can't solve problems by using the same kind of thinking we used when we created them."

Transformation has a completely different dynamic than change. Transformation doesn't accuse the past or current situation of being wrong, bad, or undesirable. Rather, transformation shifts the perspective such that what's so, or what came before, suddenly makes sense. It embraces the current reality and has it make sense in a new light. Transformation actually completes the past, makes sense of the present, and generates a future that blossoms out of what's so now. It turns what is deemed no longer useful or not right into the perfect platform or pathway to the next space. It is respectful rather than critical, affirms rather than denies, includes rather than excludes. It becomes a platform from which we take the next leap. There's a letting go of the old perceptions, and with that comes an experience of acceptance, appreciation, and even love. The sacred nature of the perfection of the universe becomes visible. While change exists primarily in time—it is time bound—transformation exists outside of time.

Transformation is a shift in the way we see the world that allows us to accept, embrace, and even celebrate what has occurred. For example, in the loss of a parent or elder loved one, you are grateful that you were able to be with that person for so long. A woman somehow comes to see her divorce newly—as unlocking her self-sufficiency, full self-expression, and independence. As a result of a transformative experience, things show up and look different, and then new behaviors and actions begin to flow from a new source. We are literally transformed, but also changed in the way we act and respond. Transformation and change work together, but they are not the same.

GEORGE FLOYD'S
TRANSFORMATIVE IMPACT

The video of the murder of George Floyd created what I would call a transformation. In the past decades, white people have seen dozens of videos of Black men being beaten and even killed by police officers. Yet, coming as it did in the middle of the pandemic year, when there was a sort of pause and everybody was paying more attention to the media and Internet news feeds, that video had a transformative impact. People braved the pandemic to march night after night in the streets, not only in the United States but throughout the world, calling for justice and for reforming policing practices.

Beyond the demonstrations, there was a complete transformation in people's willingness to call out racial injustice. There was a shift in perception and point of view such that people of all colors were impacted by that in ways that just seemed inexplicable. Prior to the video, employees of large corporations who had perhaps thought their company should hire more people of color or put them on boards of directors would not have even thought of taking that idea to their human resources department. After the video, thousands of people in organizations spoke up for diversity and inclusion.

There also began a serious discussion of reparations for African Americans. My hometown of Evanston, Illinois, authorized eligible Black families to receive up to $25,000 for house down payments or home repairs to make up for "discriminatory housing policies and practices and inaction on the city's part"— essentially the "redlining" policies that kept them from owning houses there. That would never have happened before George Floyd's murder. It didn't end police brutality, but it began the conversation about reallocating police resources to mental health and other ways of protecting the community.

Since the murder and the subsequent conviction of police officer Derek Chauvin, there have been many changes—as well as many unfulfilled promises of change—and even some backlash, causing many people to question whether a transformation actually occurred. While we have not made the progress many of us had hoped for, the blind hatred, anger, and fear that are at the heart of racism and have festered through history have been made visible. We are now speaking openly about white supremacy and are forced to address it. It has shown its true color, and only when we know what we are dealing with can we find a way to end it.

My dear friend and Pachamama Alliance colleague Rev. Deborah Johnson, who is a Black minister and activist, shares my view that it was indeed a transformative tipping point in our racist history. She says, "White people can no longer deny that for too long Black lives have not mattered. Our systems and structures have colluded to keep that hidden, so that white people won't take action. If they don't see it, they won't do anything about it. But George Floyd proved that once seen, whites rise up along with Blacks to demand justice. The apple seeds have been planted; the ground is fertile. We may have to wait for the full growth of the trees, but it is still an apple orchard."

The transformation was the result of years of educating, organizing, and mobilizing by Black Lives Matter. What began as a hashtag (#BlackLivesMatter) in 2013 initiated by three women, Alicia Garza, Patrisse Cullors, and Ayọ (Opal) Tometi, grew into a decentralized network of activists that by 2021 had become an international movement and was viewed favorably by 60 percent of Americans. These amazing women stepped into one of the most challenging moments of this century with incredible power and authority, committed that it be the breakthrough we'd been waiting for. Now, George Floyd's face is almost as recognized as Barack Obama's, and his six-year-old daughter was able to say, "My daddy changed the world."

TRANSFORMATIONAL YOUNG PEOPLE

As Rilke's opening poem indicates, there are transformational people—awakened souls who see the world differently, who begin to "move to broader deeper laws . . . demand room for bold and audacious action" and through whom "the future speaks ruthlessly."

For me, one such person was my friend and mentor Buckminster Fuller. He provided many transformational experiences for me, but perhaps the most memorable one happened during an evening when he had dinner with my family. The kids were 10, 8, and 6 at the time, and we sat around the kitchen table. Bucky loved being with children and loved the way they saw the world. At one point, my daughter, Summer, said something quite touching and beautiful that was sort of a showstopper. After she spoke, Bucky turned to Bill and me and said, "Never forget your children are your elders in universe time. They've come into a more complete, more evolved universe than you can ever understand except through their eyes."

His statement completely rearranged my molecules and my way of seeing my own children. From that moment forward, Bucky's message transformed my relationship with my kids as well as my grandchildren and all younger people. Even though young people come to me often for training and development, I have a deep respect for their fresh and evolved view of the world. I see them as my "elders in universe time," coming in with extraordinary insight and wisdom to offer to me and to the world.

I am astounded by the young people who make up generations Y and Z. In the past several years, we all have become acquainted with three young women whom I consider to be transformational leaders: Malala Yousafzai, Greta Thunberg, and Amanda Gorman. Each one at a young age chose to live a committed life,

dedicated to transforming the world through their tireless devotion to speaking the truth and galvanizing action.

Malala, generally known throughout the world by her
first name, is a Pakistani activist for female education and the
youngest Nobel Prize laureate. Born in 1997, the daughter of
an educator, she loved school, but in 2009 the Taliban were in
power in her area, and girls-only schools were closed. Malala
and her father were activists for education for girls and gained
international recognition. In 2012, she was 15 years old when
a Taliban gunman boarded her school bus shouting, "Who is
Malala?" and then shot her in the head. The murder attempt
received worldwide media coverage, and there was an outpour-
ing of both sympathy and rage, including from world leaders
and celebrities. Malala survived years of medical treatment in
England and began almost immediately to use her fame as a
platform for her commitment to schooling for girls. She started
her own foundation and became an international icon as the
wounded face of female education.

We have come to know Greta Thunberg as the unlikely but
unstoppable spokesperson for action on climate change. Greta
first learned about global warming when she was 8 years old,
and by age 11 she was so depressed that nothing significant was
being done that she started studying everything she could about
it. She also stopped eating and stopped speaking and was diag-
nosed as being on the autism spectrum. At age 15, she spent her
school days outside the Swedish Parliament holding a sign that
said *Skolstrejk för klimatet* ("School strike for climate"), which
soon inspired similar school protests that became known as Fri-
days for Future. After she spoke at the 2018 United Nations
Climate Change Conference in Poland, she ignited an international movement of millions of students worldwide calling for

more immediate and effective climate action. I love that Greta called her autism her "superpower"—the source of her passion and purpose. "The future speaks ruthlessly" through Greta, and she has lit a fire under young people that will hopefully continue to sweep the planet, demanding, in Rilke's words, "room for bold and audacious action."

At age 22, Amanda Gorman, clad in a bright yellow suit and a red hat, rocked the world at the 2021 inauguration of Joseph Biden as US president, the youngest inaugural poet ever. Reciting her poem "The Hill We Climb," she called for a new era of unity for the nation. Everything about her appearance that day was transformational—her brilliance, her beauty, her poise— setting a new standard for a new age. Here is what she told an interviewer before she spoke: "One of the preparations that I do always whenever I perform is I say a mantra to myself, which is, *I'm the daughter of black writers. We're descended from freedom fighters who broke through chains and changed the world. They call me.* And that is the way in which I prepare myself for the duty that needs to get done."

It is interesting that Amanda, raised with two siblings by a single-mother schoolteacher in Los Angeles, overcame a speech impediment and was inspired by Malala to speak out against injustice and oppression. It's clear that Amanda's vision for herself and her service to the planet is huge: she has said that she plans to run for president of the United States in 2036. I believe she has the courage, depth, and wisdom to actually accomplish that!

Like these amazing young women—our elders in universe time—there are also transformational ideas and technologies— ways of thinking, designing, and acting that offer unexpected breakthroughs and lead in new directions. Through my association with the Pachamama Alliance and Bioneers, a yearly gathering of activists and innovators, I have been exposed to the newest and most exciting approaches to healing the damage we have done to the planet and creating a regenerative future.

BIOMIMICRY: IMITATING NATURE
FOR SUSTAINABLE SUCCESS

One of the most fascinating transformational technologies is biomimicry, which means literally "imitation of the living." Drawing upon the Earth's 3.8 billion years of research and development, it is the practice of looking to Nature for inspiration to solve human design and engineering problems. Its profound insight is that Nature—plants, animals, and microorganisms—already knows what works and has sustained life on Earth from the beginning of time. This transformational way of seeing proposes an entirely new perspective on how our human creations can be efficient, sustainable, and resilient.

The principal mind behind this innovative approach is Janine Benyus, a brilliant scientist who heads the Biomimicry Institute. Janine works with businesses, corporations, and institutions throughout the world to put Nature's lessons into practice in order to "create products, processes, and policies—new ways of living—that are well-adapted to life on earth over the long haul."

I've loved Janine's TED Talks and Bioneers presentations showing how the geometry of a shell has led to the development of very small, very efficient motors, pumps, and fans; how coral reefs have inspired a new kind of concrete made from carbon dioxide; and how examining a leaf has led to better solar cells. She shows how we can mimic Nature's forms and processes, as well as entire ecosystems. Think of what is now being called the *circular economy*, based on the principles of generating no waste or polluting by-products by keeping all materials in use and regenerating natural systems.

On her website, *biomimicry.org*, Janine says, "What is most important for people to know is that a sustainable world already exists. We are just beginning to open our eyes and realize that the solutions to how do we live sustainably are already around us. It's not green design, it's just good design."

A LEGAL BREAKTHROUGH:
RIGHTS FOR NATURE

Another transformational concept that is making its way into public consciousness is Legal Rights for Nature. The Pachamama Alliance has played a key role in bringing this revolutionary idea into the conversation about how to preserve precious ecosystems. Partly out of the work of Fundación Pachamama in Ecuador, Rights of Nature was codified in the country's new constitution in 2008. This meant that the government recognized that ecosystems have the right to exist and flourish and that people can petition on behalf of those rights and require remedy to violations.

Legal Rights for Nature is a breakthrough in thinking about how to approach the protection of the web of life. It challenges our anthropocentric worldview that humans are what matters most in this world. Rivers, watersheds, forests, and other ecosystems are seen as living entities that can be defended in court with legal representation. Such an approach obviously breaks away from the traditional laws and regulatory systems that regard Nature as property and give landowners the right to damage or destroy it.

It was particularly surprising that Ecuador, a country that relies heavily on income from exploiting natural resources such as oil, timber, and minerals, should be the first nation to adopt the idea.

In 2008, the newly elected president, Rafael Correa, promised to rewrite the constitution. He called a Constituent Assembly, which was presided over by Alberto Acosta and included representatives of Indigenous communities and organizations that historically had been excluded from the political process. This is where the Pachamama Alliance's work to support and empower Indigenous activism paid off, as CONAIE, the Confederation of Indigenous Nationalities of Ecuador, lobbied for a constitution that would protect their language, culture, and sacred lands. Indigenous activism played a major role in the passage of this radical new constitution.

Rights of Nature has just begun to set new precedents that impact Ecuador's environmental policies and promises to enable the government to block extractive industries in areas of high biodiversity. It has been applied elsewhere in a number of legal disputes. At this writing, other countries, including Colombia, Bolivia, Nepal, India, and Turkey, as well as several municipalities in the United States, have used the idea to protect rivers, forests, and other ecosystems. Rights of Nature is an idea whose time is coming, standing in the wings of transformational efforts to protect and regenerate Mother Earth—Pachamama.

Transformation is taking place everywhere on earth in micro and macro ways. These small and large breakthroughs are underreported and sometimes invisible. However, conscious and committed human beings everywhere are generating new possibilities and profound new ways of being that are at the cutting edge of an evolutionary leap.

CHAPTER 6

Context: The Power of Story

*For peoples, generally, their story of the universe and
the human role in the universe is their primary source of
intelligibility and value. The deepest crises experienced by
any society are those moments of change when the story
becomes inadequate for meeting the survival demands of
a present situation.*

—THOMAS BERRY

Consider a woman, Emily let's say, who is approaching 45 years old and feels ill and exhausted. She is nauseous and achy, can't focus, and is overwhelmed emotionally. Emily is terrified that something is wrong with her, and her friends finally talk her into going to the doctor. She is crying and shaking as she recounts her symptoms, fearful of what the doctor will say. After examining her, the doctor announces, "You're pregnant." Emily, who has believed she was infertile after years of trying to conceive, is jubilant. In a few seconds, those two words shifted the context of her illness and transformed her life. Suddenly, she has a completely new context for her bodily experience as well as a new future. She's finally going to have the family she's always dreamed of. The glorious future reaches back and transforms the past—a new life is growing within her, and she has shifted from fear to feeling honored and elated.

We have all experienced times when something happened that changed everything, be it a tragedy or what we call a gift from the Universe. But often the shift must happen within ourselves—how we choose to interpret something differently and begin to speak about it in new ways. How we language something—our inner and outer conversations about it—enables us to shift the paradigm we are living in. All of these words—conversation, context, paradigm, narrative—boil down to the story we tell ourselves and others.

It has become clear to me that we don't necessarily live in the reality of the world. We live in the conversation we have about the reality of the world. We don't necessarily live in our relationships or our health or our marriage or our job. We live in the conversation we have about our relationships, our marriage, our job, our health. And that story, that narrative, that conversation, is malleable. We don't have absolute omnipotence over the circumstances of our lives, but we do have absolute omnipotence over how we respond to them—the thoughts in our head about them, the stories we listen to, and what we speak about to others. Over that we have total power. That conversation belongs to us. A new conversation—or languaging something differently—shifts the context, shifts how it shows up, and ultimately shifts the action we take.

The way to transform any situation is by *shifting the context*—the container, the frame, the conversation about it—essentially, *telling a new story*. A new story reshapes content, actually redefines reality. Illuminating the power of story to heal, to inspire, and to create possibility is one of the most powerful things I have learned in my life and has been a major expression of my work of deep engagement with global issues.

THE HUNGER PROJECT
TELLS A NEW STORY

I began to learn about the power of story in my early work with The Hunger Project: it was the key to what Werner Erhard sought to bring to the global conversation about hunger and starvation. What the project aimed to transform was the context in which hunger and starvation were held in our global society. When the project began, hunger was seen as an inevitable and incurable tragedy with helpless, hopeless victims, and the best that could be done was to alleviate their suffering. That was really the context or the condition that characterized the issue of hunger at the end of the 20th century. Much of the hunger-response community was focused on providing direct food aid to the hungry and starving, an action that provided temporary relief but ended up driving down the local food economy and making people dependent rather than empowered to feed themselves.

The Hunger Project generated a new story, a new context, that humanity could actually end world hunger by the year 2000. It was a bold idea, never really declared before. It seemed almost ridiculous at first, like saying you could end rain. But the declaration was not a pie-in-the-sky dream. Buckminster Fuller was among many scientists who confirmed that indeed the world already produced enough food to feed everyone on the planet. Scarcity was not the issue. Commitment was.

Once people began to see the possibility of ending hunger, a new world opened up. You couldn't work on it in the same way. You couldn't be satisfied with just alleviating suffering. Now there was a need for a measurement of hunger as well as progress in ending it. The infant mortality rate then came into view as an indicator of society-wide hunger, and the goal was to reduce it as quickly as possible. Rather than measuring a tragedy, reducing infant mortality became a way to see progress toward a feasible goal.

The Hunger Project declared that ending hunger was an idea whose time had come. It was Victor Hugo who said, "All the forces in the world are not so powerful as an idea whose time has come." But what causes an idea's time to come? For Werner Erhard and Bucky Fuller, the creation of a new context was a function of the personal commitment of a human being. Individuals could be involved in ending hunger by personally committing to that context. Indeed, it was my commitment to The Hunger Project that shifted the context of my life from the comfort and happiness of Lynne Twist to making a difference as a global activist for the end of hunger.

In his remarkable essay "An Idea Whose Time Has Come" (known to many as "The Hunger Project Source Document"), Werner explains context:

There isn't a person reading this who does not know the power of context in his or her own life. Whether you were conscious of it or not at the time, there have been times when you created a context in your life. As a consequence of your doing so, suddenly things started to work: That which previously did not work, that which was stuck and

not moving, suddenly began to move and start working.
When you create a context, it's not that you are now doing
something very much different from what you were doing
before or even that you now know something very much
different from what you knew before. It is that there is a
shift in the climate, the space (specifically, the context) in
which you work, that makes things suddenly workable.

COMMITMENT
CREATES CONTEXT

When President Kennedy said in 1961, "I believe that this nation should commit itself to achieving the goal, before this decade is out, of landing a man on the moon and returning him safely to the Earth," he created a context. Imagine if he had said, "We're going to do everything we can to try to get a man on the moon." There's no context to that; it's just a good idea that may or may not work. It's not a commitment, just a rearranging of the circumstances. On the other hand, Kennedy made a declaration, a commitment. Generating a context comes from commitment, and a context really worth creating derives from the deepest sense of who we are, from our power to create, our power to generate.

When we think of people we admire and who have made a significant difference in the world—people like Susan B. Anthony, Martin Luther King Jr., Mahatma Gandhi, Jane Goodall, and Nelson Mandela—they are people who took a stand that was so inspiring that it created an entirely new context. And within that context, the content eventually started to line up with what they were standing for. In the presence of a

powerful stand, people and circumstances change and reconfig-
ure, and the world appears differently.

I had a powerful experience with this process in the after-
math of the Bernie Madoff investment scandal in 2008. His
Ponzi scheme—paying previous investors with money from
new investors—involved thousands of people who lost billions
of dollars of savings. I happened to be well acquainted with a
number of those people who were financially and emotionally
devastated. Some very dear friends were part of a support group
of about 22 families in and around New York City who were
brutally hurt and called themselves "the Madoff Victims." Some
had read *The Soul of Money* and asked me to help raise money for
people who were about to lose their homes and also to consult
with their group.

In a series of conference calls, I suggested a shift in language
and context: Could they see themselves as survivors rather than
victims? Could they embrace the idea that they would survive
and ultimately thrive out of this experience? It was a lot to ask,
but they were game to look deeply now at their relationship with
money, and also their relationships with each other. Out of a new
sense of connection and commitment, they began collaborating
with each other in remarkable ways. The family that ran a raft
of Mercedes repair shops offered free car services. The Brooklyn
teacher who lost her entire life savings started schooling the kids
of families who could no longer afford private schools. A broke
accountant did people's taxes. A masseuse gave massages for free.
The group gathered at potluck dinners. They created a kind of
community that many of them had never known—a community of sharing and gifting. They engaged deeply with each other
about how they might re-create their lives and their businesses.

THE ROBBINSES'
TRANSFORMATIONAL JOURNEY

My dear friends John Robbins and his son, Ocean Robbins, had a particularly powerful experience of not only surviving but thriving as a result of that shift in context regarding Madoff's impact. John is the author of nine books that connect diet, health, the environment, and animal rights, including the international bestseller *Diet for a New America*. Groomed to take over his family business, the Baskin-Robbins ice cream chain, John left a fortune behind and set out to educate people worldwide about how food and food production impact the health of people and the planet. Ocean joined in the work, heading up a nonprofit while also being father to special needs twins.

Through his bestselling books, John had accumulated not a fortune, but still a healthy sufficiency of money, all of which his money manager had invested with Madoff. When the Madoff scam was revealed in 2008, the Robbins family lost all of their savings at a time when their home was also mortgaged to the hilt. Gifts from the many people whose lives they had touched enabled them to survive without losing their home, but Ocean realized that they needed a new path to financial sustainability. He left his nonprofit, Youth for Environmental Sanity (YES), to create a new business promoting a whole-foods, plant-powered diet and supporting healthy, ethical, organic food production and consumption. He started learning about business and online marketing, and at the end of 2011, father and son launched the online Food Revolution Network.

The network broke new ground with "telesummits"—online interviews with top experts in the food movement—and their impact grew exponentially. In the ensuing 10 years, the Food

Revolution Network grew to serve 750,000 active members, millions of summit participants, and 10 million blog visitors a year. Most important, their programs are having a life-changing impact on those people and helping to change the course of the planet by bringing about systemic change in our food systems. The mission statement of the Food Revolution Network is "healthy, ethical, sustainable food for all"—not just for those who can afford it!

Both John and Ocean now recognize the catalytic effect of the Madoff tragedy on their lives and the personal choice to embrace a context of personal power. John told me,

> *I realized I had to get off being a victim, and the way I did that was with gratitude—not make it up, not pretend, 'Oh, I'm grateful for Madoff.' I was not. But I didn't want that man's actions to dominate and define my life anymore. I realized that what I had done all these years was real, and it wasn't negated by this at all. And I got confirmation for that, right? From the remarkable number of gifts that we received and from the success we have had.*

And Ocean says,

> *From my perspective, without the Madoff push I would not have left the nonprofit, I don't think. I would not have passionately pursued business and looked at online marketing and discovered all of this possibility without the catalyst that was evoked for me from that tragedy. So for me, the biggest lessons are that sometimes tragedy can evoke opportunity. Sometimes. Not that it doesn't hurt, but it can still be a catalyst for something. And with all the pain*

that's in the world right now, with all that's broken, we as
a species had better learn how to make something out of it,
because if we stay in complaining and cynicism and fear and
keep our hearts closed, then there isn't much hope for our
species. But if we can find some way to allow the immensity
of the pain to open us, not shut us down, but expand our
capacity to respond with the best of who we are, then maybe
something worthwhile can come of it.

And that's what my life's about.

That is what my committed life is about as well. The power of story and of language has been a prominent theme in my work as an activist. Over the years, I have created the context of seeing myself as a *pro-activist*. I honor and respect all activists and protests against injustice, but for myself I made the distinction of focusing my activism on what I am *for* rather than what I am *against*. I am not naive; I can certainly see that the status quo is not healthy, but rather than attacking, I stand firmly in the vision to hospice the death of obstacles and midwife the birth of the world I want to see. In these times, it is ever more clear how narratives actually generate actions—sometimes disturbing, upsetting action; sometimes positive, powerful action. If we aim to live a committed life, it is our responsibility to listen for and generate conversations and contexts that empower ourselves and others.

CHANGING THE DREAM OF
THE MODERN WORLD

At the beginning of this century, the Pachamama Alliance created a program called Awakening the Dreamer, Changing the Dream. It began as a daylong symposium and evolved over the years into an online course experienced by hundreds of thousands of people throughout the world. One of the tenets of the Awakening the Dreamer program is that people in the modern world are living in some sort of trance: We are sleepwalking through a consumerist culture based on extraction, consumption, and disposability. We want more of everything, thinking it will bring us happiness or at least satisfaction. Instead, this paradigm of infinite growth on a finite planet is destroying our environment and wreaking havoc on social justice as well as human fulfillment.

Changing the story is critical to changing the dream. The Awakening the Dreamer experience pierced through the unconsciousness and aimed to wake people up from the trance—to shift the context of mindless consumption and the denial and apathy it created. It had people examine the Old Story of humanity based on the illusion of separateness, and on scarcity and competition. It presented a New Story of interconnectedness, sufficiency, and cooperation—what we called "an environmentally sustainable, spiritually fulfilling, socially just human presence on this planet." It called forth new thinking about who are we, really? What is ours to do, to create? What are our true dreams for the world, and what is our role in creating the future we want—a future where we love life—we love each other, we love the Earth, we love other species, and we live in total respect for future generations?

SHIFTING CONTEXT
FROM "TO" TO "FOR"

A new conversation is crucial to a new future. We need to stimulate our imaginations and generate new visions. The trance we've been living in for so long—that we became numb to—is now actually under siege or in a kind of collapse. All of the institutions of society are falling apart right in front of our eyes. So, the trance has been shaken, and we are awakening from our numbness and denial. All of our systems are failing and need to be regenerated, and in a way, that's good because we have to wake up and create the new world.

Yet often when we wake up, we fall into a sense of fear and anxiety about the future. When we really know what is happening, we risk being caught in negativity. Why is this happening to us? My dear friend Paul Hawken has given me a new context for this question, one that has opened me to new possibilities of understanding and action. Paul is the creator of Project Drawdown, an extraordinary vision of how humanity can begin to reverse global warming by 2060; and is the author of two landmark books: *Drawdown: The Most Comprehensive Plan Ever Proposed to Reverse Global Warming*, and *Regeneration: Ending the Climate Crisis in One Generation*. In *Drawdown*, Paul wrote,

> *The buildup of greenhouse gases we experience today occurred in the absence of human understanding; our ancestors were innocent of the damage they were doing. That can tempt us to believe that global warming is something that is happening to us—that we are victims of a fate that was determined by actions that precede us. If we change the preposition, and consider that global warming is happening for us—an atmospheric transformation that inspires us to change and reimagine everything we make and do—we begin to live in a different world. We take 100 percent responsibility and stop blaming others. We see global*

warming not as an inevitability but as an invitation to build, innovate, and effect change, a pathway that awakens creativity, compassion, and genius.

That invitation to change prepositions from *to* to *for* has inspired me to see all sorts of situations differently. When we live in the story that the circumstances we face, whether positive or negative, are happening to us, we are the victims and have no power. When we live in a story that the circumstances are happening for us, we are constantly open to learning, developing, and receiving the constant feedback that inspires and catalyzes us to evolve and grow.

CHAPTER 7

The Magic of Possibility

Some men see things as they are, and ask why.
I dream of things that never were, and ask why not.
—ROBERT F. KENNEDY

It always seems impossible until it's done.
—NELSON MANDELA

At the height of the COVID-19 pandemic, a friend shared with me how depressed he had felt about all that he could not do: "I can't see my grandchildren; we can't have friends over; I can't go out without a mask; there's no place to go and nothing to do . . . I can't, I can't, I can't . . ."

He said he felt imprisoned and shut down until he started thinking about what he could do: "I can have dinner with my wife every single night; I can work in the garden; I can read those books that have been stacked up next to my bed for years that I've never read; I can cook, which I love to do; I can spend some time rearranging my clothing and getting rid of stuff; I can practice the guitar, I can spend more time meditating . . ."

Focusing on what he could do created a huge possibility. It opened up a world of things he'd always wanted to do but never felt he had the time, the space, or the environment to pursue. He said, "It was just amazing how much this shift in perspective changed my life. Once I paid attention to what could be—I recalibrated from I can't to I can—the possibilities were endless. Now I'm inspired by all the stuff I can do!"

If you set out to live a committed life and to keep your commitments, it's essential that you know how to create possibility. I refer to "possibility" not just as a conglomerate of options but as a mindset—a way of thinking and interacting with the world that sustains, inspires, and empowers you. My colleague Frances Moore Lappé calls this being a "possibilist"—someone who sees the world through a mental lens of what can be and what could be rather than what they perceive to be happening right now.

Seeing possibility and speaking about it is one of my superpowers. The transformation I've been committed to all my life is to pierce through apathy and resignation, to touch people and inspire them to see what's possible, and to generate and live in a context of possibility. Maybe I was born on a sunny day or under lucky stars, but I've always been an advocate for turning complaints into commitments. I've gotten really good at it because I practice it all the time. It's a daily practice, sometimes an hourly practice, to turn negative thoughts into positive ones.

GROUNDED OPTIMISM

One of the things that happen when you wake up is you realize you're swimming in negative conversations, in negative media

coverage, and in people's complaints about the world, perhaps
even your own. And those negative conversations, which are a
dime a dozen and everywhere you look, are conversations that
keep us stuck in a victim story, as though we can't do anything
about these things. We see ourselves as victims of the circumstances of the pandemic, the political system, the economy, climate change, the health care system, and even our own worries
about the world.

We may think we are just being "realistic" about the state
of the world, but it's important to recognize that negativity and
cynicism disempower us. The world is transformed by thinkers
and activists who look for and stand for possibility; they take the
long view, they can tolerate uncertainty, and they recognize that
cynicism only serves the status quo. As author Alex Steffen says,
"Optimism is a political act. Those who benefit from the status
quo are perfectly happy for us to think nothing is going to get
any better. In fact, these days, cynicism is obedience."

I have often used a wonderful phrase from Rev. Michael
Beckwith, "Worry is a form of negative prayer." When you
worry, your psychic energy, your "prayer," is going toward what
you don't want. It's easy to think of yourself as a victim—to be
upset or angry or ashamed and fall into despair. What's difficult
and challenging—and often takes moral courage—is to look
for what's working that no one is paying attention to and to
shine a light on progress that is being made or a larger purpose
that is being served. As you shift the conversation in your own
mind, you can then have the conversations you have with others become a source of appreciation and gratitude. To be someone who looks for possibility is a very, very critical job. Positive
thinking and possibility are not the same thing, but they're
related—and they relate as well to optimism. I refer to myself as

a committed optimist or a grounded optimist. Grounded optimism is something we need and something that everyone has access to.

Being a possibilist or a grounded optimist doesn't mean being naive or Pollyannaish. It's not about being in denial or stepping over things that aren't working. It's not about magical thinking or even positive thinking. Sometimes positive thinking just ignores what's not working or what's dark or unethical. Possibility doesn't do that; it includes and acknowledges obstacles and the shadow side and allows them to be. Rather than ignore the dark side, it requires you to pay astute attention to what you might consider to be negative. Just as the lotus is born out of the mud, so is possibility.

When Donald Trump got elected and began his term of office, my personal view of him was that he was dominating, disrespectful, and reckless. It was very hard for me to create possibility out of that. I kept thinking, "How can I, for myself first, and then for other people, see the possibility in these four years of what seems to be toxic leadership?" I really had to work at it, and then I realized that this man was bringing to visibility all the dark forces simmering under the surface of our patriarchal society—white supremacy, racism, misogyny, domination, worship of money. All of this came into view because it's time to deal with what's unresolved and totally off in our country. We can't pretend it's not here anymore: this man is going to make sure we see this darkness so that we can begin to handle it. And that is what has happened: many sectors of society, President Biden, the Congress, businesses, nongovernmental organizations, and activists of all kinds are tackling some of the darkest and most difficult aspects of our society that were invisible until the Trump administration made them so blatant.

Currently, we are witnessing unprecedented attacks on the fundamentals of democracy: the right to vote and the sanctity of elections. After hundreds of years as a beacon of democracy, the United States is being challenged internally in ways that are shaking the very foundation of our nation. We can't gloss over this breakdown of democracy: we have to be vigilant and willing to take courageous action. Our fears are realistic, but we can't be paralyzed by them. As Eleanor Roosevelt said, "Courage is more exhilarating than fear, and in the long run it's easier."

HOW POSSIBILITY TRANSFORMS

Fear is often our first reaction to obstacles, and free-floating anxiety can cripple us and keep us from taking action. So this is the magic of creating possibility: it breaks people out of their unexamined assumptions of what can and cannot happen. It transforms the present and opens new vistas and ways of being in the future. I remember the moment in 2009 when President Obama first walked up the White House steps with his wife and two daughters. That moment changed the game for every African American in our country, as well as Black people everywhere, and a new future was possible. When 22-year-old Amanda Gorman walked up to the podium at the Biden inauguration and read her poem "The Hill We Climb," her eloquence, clarity, and beauty created a new possibility for little Black girls everywhere.

I have had the profound blessing of being interviewed by Oprah Winfrey, someone I consider to be a shining light of possibility. Her vast audiences have been treated to the most heartwarming accounts of near-miracles in people's lives, but she has also never been afraid to take on dark topics and transform how they are seen. Whether it was Michael Jackson's alleged abuse of young children or the unjust incarceration of the Central Park Five, she approaches the truth through the lens of compassion and what can be learned from tragedy. I think this is what has made her so popular: her ability to illuminate even the toughest situations with love and hope.

Jane Goodall is another possibilist who imbues all of her interactions with an empowering perspective. Her work with chimpanzees in Africa established the possibility of consciousness and communication in these primates and was a revelation for the scientific community. Up into her 80s (until COVID-19 grounded her in 2020), she was traveling the world and speaking 300 days a year, committed to instilling in her audiences a sense of hope for the future. Indeed, five of her more than two dozen books have the word hope in the title, including her most recent 2021 publication of *The Book of Hope: A Survival Guide for Trying Times.*

As we consider the magic of possibility, we have to keep in mind that the first step in keeping a commitment is acknowledging what's so now and what's in the way. What is the resistance to what you are seeking to achieve? If you are breaking into new territory, you will almost certainly get pushback from the status quo. If, instead of being threatened by it, you can see it as useful feedback, then you can learn from it. It's not something to argue with, it's something to embrace and understand. If you consider your commitment to be a physical building with various offices, the office of "It Can't Be Done" should occupy a ground-floor space—a place you visit and commune with. Fighting or resisting the resistance only strengthens it, while allowing and encountering it makes space for transformation.

FROM RESISTANCE TO VISION

Since 1996, the Pachamama Alliance has worked with the Indigenous people of the Ecuadorean Amazon to stop the exploitation of the rainforest that threatens their land, livelihood, and culture. Clear-cutting of forests for timber and toxic mining for gold and other metals have done significant damage, but oil production has been especially devastating, polluting land and waterways and sickening local people, particularly in the northern area of Ecuador's Amazon.

For years, the Achuar people of the southern Amazon region of Ecuador have worked in partnership with the Pachamama Alliance and local partner Fundación Pachamama to prevent oil development in their territories. The organization and continuing resistance by the Indigenous people have been amazingly successful. After a succession of attempts at incursions by international oil companies, no new oil development has occurred in this pristine region in the past 25 years. That is nothing short of miraculous, given that the petroleum industry has provided about 45 percent of Ecuador's budget and that China has loaned billions of dollars to be repaid in oil.

Over the years, the tension between the government and Indigenous organizations fighting to stop oil expansion ebbed and flowed, but as oil prices rose, the relationship became more and more antagonistic. Responsible for feeding and supporting 18 million people, the government needed oil income and grew increasingly hostile toward the Indigenous resistance to new oil projects. Then, at the end of 2013, oil prices dropped dramatically, and at the same time the international community was beginning to mobilize around addressing climate change. Oil no longer looked like a viable long-term economic alternative for the region. Something else was called for.

Belen Paez, director of Fundación Pachamama, and my husband Bill Twist, CEO of the Pachamama Alliance, took the opportunity to forge a new approach. How could they work with the government to find alternatives to extractive industries like oil—especially since fossil fuels need to be phased out to address climate change? What could enable the government to take care of their people as well as preserve the rainforest? It's clear that a new economic model is needed now and for the long-term future. So rather than just fighting the status quo, they focused on educating the government and challenging themselves and the Indigenous movement to come up with new possibilities for the future economic development of the country. The pushback was generative: it allowed collaborative and creative juices to flow. The Indigenous community began to see new possibilities and to feel the agency to make them happen.

What evolved was a new vision that is one of the most innovative and important conservation programs on earth, the Amazon Sacred Headwaters Initiative. The territory called the Sacred Headwaters encompasses 85 million acres of Amazonian rainforest in Ecuador and Peru. Located at the headwaters of the Napo, Pastaza, and Marañon river basins, it is one of the most biodiverse regions on the planet, home to vast varieties of animals as well as plants whose medicinal uses are just being discovered. The forest itself is vital to regulating the planet's climate, breathing in carbon dioxide and breathing out oxygen. It is also the home to 30 Indigenous nationalities who have miraculously come together to call for the permanent protection of this precious global resource. The Initiative is calling for halting the expansion of extractive industries, making the area off-limits to industrial-scale development and establishing it as a sanctuary for Nature and for humanity.

In a remarkable participatory process, led by Atossa Soltani, the founder of Amazon Watch and now the director of global strategy for the Amazon Sacred Headwaters Initiative, Indigenous organizations and their NGO supporters, including the Pachamama Alliance, have developed a bioregional plan that ensures that the area will be governed in accordance with Indigenous principles of cooperation and harmony with all life. The plan includes strategies for the sustainable development of new economic products, education, intercultural health care, transportation, renewable energy, forest conservation, governance, and more. The Indigenous residents envision continuing to live in harmony with Nature, pursuing their livelihood in the forest while safeguarding the vital organs of the Earth for all of life. All this will be building toward a 20-year vision that sees the Sacred Headwaters region as a model of a new kind of ecological civilization that honors and regenerates life and biodiversity and contributes to the reversal of global warming.

None of this would have come to pass if we were just fighting the oil companies or fighting the government. But in paying attention to the pushback and creating a possibility for long-term protection of the forest, we generated a project like no other. Now the process involves working with the governments of Ecuador and Peru to come up with new solutions, new economic models, that will enable those governments to do a better job of taking care of all of their people as well as preserving their natural resources.

POSSIBILITY AND THE CLIMATE CRISIS

In the realm of creating possibility, no one is more active, effective, or inspiring than Paul Hawken. Since his youth working in the Civil Rights Movement through the past decades as a businessman, environmentalist, author, and activist, Paul has been a possibilist par excellence, describing what is happening now and envisioning what needs to happen next. In 2013, frustrated at the lack of possibility in the climate change conversation, Paul initiated Project Drawdown, which brought together 200 researchers and advisers to model the most substantive solutions to reverse global warming. In terms of climate, "drawdown is the point at which greenhouse gas concentrations in the atmosphere level off and begin to decline on a year-to-year basis." It's a milestone in reversing climate change and eventually reducing global average temperatures.

In 2017, Paul and his collaborators published the groundbreaking book *Drawdown: The Most Comprehensive Plan Ever Proposed to Reverse Global Warming.* It is the most comprehensive plan because it is the *only* plan that has been proposed to achieve a *reversal* of global warming. It does not make wrong the plethora of approaches to combating and mitigating climate change, but it proposes an entirely new way of thinking—not only how to reduce carbon emissions but how to prevent them and sequester carbon for a net zero carbon future. It looks beyond the technical solutions like solar and wind power to social solutions as well, like family planning and educating women and girls. Project Drawdown (*drawdown.org*) continues to be a source of great information about the science behind climate solutions and how to engage with them.

In 2021, Paul published *Regeneration: Ending the Climate Crisis in One Generation.* In this follow-on to *Drawdown*, he looks through another lens at the climate crisis: it is not a science problem but a human problem. He describes *regeneration* as "putting life at the center of every action and decision" with regard to all of our current systems—human as well as ecological. The book looks at oceans, forests, agricultural land, and wilderness as well as cities, food, energy, and a range of industries, calling for a new human relationship with Nature based on the interconnectedness of all things and for immediate worldwide collective action at what he calls "a watershed moment in history."

Paul says that agency—a sense of power to take effective action—emerges from individuals who see the possibilities for regenerating human well-being, health, justice, and security as well as cutting carbon emissions. With *Regeneration*, as with *Drawdown*, Paul's commitment to possibility transforms resignation and despair into energy for inspired, committed action. If we fear the future, that stress is a signal that we need to get into action to address current human needs, and that is a job for individuals as well as governments and every sector of society. "If we are going to save the world from the threat of global warming," he says, "we need to create a world worth saving."

Seeing possibility—coming from a place of grounded optimism—is life changing, life altering. It's an act of profound responsibility and even integrity. Possibility isn't something that is there waiting to be discovered. We have to generate it. It can't be an opinion or point of view that we have or a position we take; it must be a stand that comes from the depths of who we are. Generating possibility is a creative act, an act of commitment and of love. It's a muscle that needs to be worked and developed, and it takes practice! Being a possibilist—a grounded, committed optimist—is a job, really, an accountability. It's our responsibility to create possibility for ourselves, for our children, for the people and creatures we love, and for the planet.

CHAPTER 8

Breakdown into Breakthrough

*Every adversity, every failure, and every heartache
carries with it the Seed of an equivalent or greater Benefit.
But you have to look for the seed and water it.*
—NAPOLEON HILL

For more than 20 years, The Hunger Project was my life. I lived and breathed it—I could say I slept it too, but I didn't sleep that much, so demanding was my schedule of global travel and fundraising. I was so devoted that I said, perhaps hundreds of times to hundreds of people, that I would never leave The Hunger Project. "I've been here since the beginning, and I will be here until the end." And by that I meant until the end of hunger. In essence, I was giving my word never to leave—which led to the major breakdown (and then breakthrough) of my life.

I was devoted not only to the organization, but also to the two people most responsible for The Hunger Project—the founder, Werner Erhard, and the executive director, Joan Holmes. I was in awe of them both, and I saw myself as their humble servant. Yet at the same time—the early 1990s—I was being recognized and called out into a wider world of service. I was invited to join the board of directors of the Institute of Noetic Sciences, a think tank founded by astronaut Edgar Mitchell exploring the intersection of science and spirituality. Over the years 1995 to 1999 I collaborated with Jim Garrison in co-leading the State of the World Forum, a yearly gathering of world leaders to envision the 21st century. I joined the board of the Fetzer Institute, whose unique mission introduced me to spiritual icons and practices. I was interacting with fascinating people, and I began to be engaged in a world that wasn't The Hunger Project. A new world was opening up to me, and I was experiencing a new sense of myself—an individuation process that was making my work with The Hunger Project feel somewhat unsettling.

MY OWN BREAKDOWN
INTO BREAKTHROUGH

In 1995 came the journey to the Ecuadorean Amazon and the encounter with the Achuar people, whose call had captivated my husband Bill and pulled at me as well. It was I, after all, who had received the mystical visions that called us to the rainforest where what was to become the Pachamama Alliance was launched. I was thrilled that Bill, whose interest at the time had mainly been focused on business and yacht racing, now had a vision of a commitment that would soon envelop his life. I wanted to join him, but it was inconceivable to me that I would ever leave The Hunger Project. By this time, the organization had moved its headquarters to New York City, and a number of the original staff had left, but a few of us remained in San Francisco, where I still managed the global fundraising efforts.

Then I got sick—very, very sick. Although it took some months to determine the cause, it eventually became clear that I had malaria, contracted in my travels in Africa. I was completely immobilized for about nine months, so ill that I couldn't work. I couldn't even be on conference calls and had a hard time talking to Bill and the kids. I was totally despondent, lying in bed day and night fearful that I would never be well again.

Finally, a radical cleansing program brought me back, but meanwhile, The Hunger Project had found a way to replace me. When I was well enough to return, it didn't seem that I was needed, but I wanted to stay involved. I asked for a position on the board, which Joan Holmes declined. I was heartbroken and adrift. The Hunger Project had been my identity, and I didn't know who I was without it. I was afraid that I had no value without it, no value of my own. I wanted to leave, but I had given my word that I would be there till the end. How could I abandon ending hunger to embrace a new mission of protecting the rainforest? I felt like my life commitment was in total breakdown.

What finally enabled me to make the break was an experience I had on a Hunger Project trip to Ghana in 1998. I was sitting with a group of old men and one old woman on barren, dusty ground in the midst of a desert, no grass or trees in sight, discussing how to deal with their plight. They must have been in their 70s and 80s. They recounted to me how they had grown up in a rainforest—"but now it's gone, all gone for 40 years now. The trees were cut down, and we've had to adjust to living in this arid climate. Life is hard, and that's why we are hungry." I was shocked because I had never thought of Ghana as having a rainforest. After this experience, I did some research and found that many of the places where I had been working on hunger and poverty—Namibia, Zimbabwe, India, Bangladesh—had once been verdant rainforests supporting thriving communities. The loss of the forest had created a cascading loss of biodiversity and agriculture.

My breakthrough came when I realized, "Oh my God, by working on preserving the Amazon rainforest, I'm still working on ending hunger! If we don't stop the destruction of that great forest, it will become another desert. I'm moving from trying to resolve the consequences of deforestation to preventing defor-estation. I'm moving to working on the source of the hunger problem and stopping it before it happens. I am still a person of my word." A huge weight was lifted, and that reframing made it okay for me to let go of The Hunger Project and give my whole heart and soul to the Pachamama Alliance and other causes.

A CALL TO CREATE

An authentic commitment that inspires and motivates you can also often generate a breakdown. What you're committed to doesn't exist, and you're living in what's so, the status quo, not what will be. You have to invent ways of being that you haven't known before, find resources you don't even know exist, create relationships where there are none. It looks like a panoply of problems to be solved, when it's actually a call to create.

My breakdown into breakthrough happened over a period of two years, but the process can also occur over months or days. Things start to go wrong, often with cascading effects and emotions—embarrassment, disappointment, uncertainty, failure, heartbreak, grief, despair, and depression. The emotional impact needs to be experienced and expressed, to be fully almost squeezed out of us. Once we move through this feeling state, we can begin to see what Napoleon Hill says about failure and heartache holding the seed of a breakthrough even greater than the breakdown.

In order to consciously navigate a breakdown into breakthrough, one needs to really look for the seeds of the breakthrough, to have the will, the courage, the wonder, and the curiosity to engage with some deep questions: What is the feedback? What is the teaching here? What is the message when one door closes and another door opens? Every gift of the universe is only a gift if it's received. Usually what gets revealed is a possibility that we never knew was there. And if we water that possibility, if we're looking for it, connect to it, and nourish and fertilize it, it can be the source of a breakthrough that launches us into a new space, even a new life. It's a bit like the process our bodies go through in lifting weights to build muscles—the muscle is stressed until it breaks down, and then the body rebuilds it so it is even bigger and stronger.

For most of us, every disappointment, every heartbreak, every breakdown is the opportunity for a breakthrough and an evolutionary leap in life. If you have that context and that way of seeing the world, you can handle anything—or almost anything. Of course, I say that as a person who is a white American who has had every possible privilege. I want to be clear that this may not be true for people who are marginalized and oppressed—who truly are victims of a dysfunctional society. We can't equate the loss of a child to unjustified police violence or the years in prison for a crime you did not commit with a "breakdown." It takes uncommon courage in some settings to even find the possibility of a breakthrough, so I don't want to make this sound like it's easy. Of course, there are people who do turn incredibly difficult circumstances into opportunities to grow, learn, and serve others, but I don't want to set up the expectation that all breakdown circumstances are equal or can always be transformed.

Some of our greatest leaders and the most admired people in history are people who've gone through difficult, uncomfortable, and even horrendous experiences. I think of my wonderful sisters who have won the Nobel Peace Prize. All of them have had transformational breakdowns in their lives. Leymah Gbowee of Liberia was only 17 years old when she was suddenly thrust into being responsible for a large family. The multiyear war that raged in her country reached her town, and her parents were unable to return home. Violent mobs roamed the streets raping, plundering, and killing people, and Leymah was suddenly responsible for protecting her brothers and sisters and a large household of people. She went from a wild-child teenager who had her mind on boys and having fun to being a protector of many people. In the years that followed, that experience forged her strength and courage and enabled her to become an extraordinary young leader. It was Leymah who organized thousands of women—mothers, girls, and grandmothers—to stop the brutal atrocities and horrendous, vicious war in Liberia. For that courageous work, she won the Nobel Peace Prize in 2011.

VAN JONES:
WATERING THE SEEDS

Several of the stories I have shared are of people who turned breakdowns into breakthroughs—like John and Ocean Robbins in chapter 6. In chapter 4, you met Van Jones, who managed to wrestle a breakthrough out of a breakdown with the First Step Act prison reform legislation. I return to Van with another story that happened a bit earlier in his life and illustrates the candor and courage it takes to water the seeds of breakthrough.

I came to know Van when he headed the Ella Baker Center for Human Rights in Oakland, California, where he was instrumental in promoting prison and policing reform. When our Pachamama Alliance team was creating the Awakening the Dreamer, Changing the Dream Symposium, we declared that the purpose of this educational course was to "bring forth an environmentally sustainable, spiritually fulfilling, socially just human presence on this planet." We white folks knew a good bit about sustainability and spirituality, but not so much about social justice. Van was already connecting the dots between the environmental movement and the social justice movement, and he generously responded to our request to become our teacher and mentor. He became one of our primary speakers in the Awakening the Dreamer program videos—wise, eloquent, and extremely inspiring.

About this time, he authored a book called *The Green Collar Economy: How One Solution Can Fix Our Two Biggest Problems*, which proposed a "green new deal" that would address the United States' ecological and economic crises by creating thousands of low- and medium-skilled jobs that would help conserve energy and create a "green wave that lifts all boats." It was the first environmental book written by an African American to make the *New York Times* bestsellers list.

By 2009, Van had become one of *Time* magazine's 100 Most Influential People in the World, and newly elected President Barack Obama brought him to the White House to become special adviser for green jobs, enterprise, and innovation. It was his dream job, but almost immediately, Van was criticized by the conservative media. Glenn Beck of Fox News launched an all-out attack on Van as a communist and a radical who hated Republicans and believed that the 9/11 attacks were an inside job. It was a vicious smear campaign with no grounding in truth, but given the tense political climate, Van felt compelled to resign his position.

After a decade of success, he was suddenly adrift, ostracized by people and organizations who had previously courted him. He was shattered. Of his breakdown, Van says, "I was clinically depressed for a year after that. I thought my life was over. Up to that time, my life had been a fight, but I had been able to win pretty much every round—going from the edge of a small town in rural west Tennessee to getting into Yale Law School to setting up my own organization—it was all hard, but it kept having these happy endings. And then suddenly, a massive defeat. All of my achievements, my proof points, were external, and I had to put myself back together. I had to literally start over, but it meant that I was going to have to rise independently. I wasn't going to be able to be a part of the Obama machine and just rise with it. I was outside of it now, on my own."

Van worked on himself, seeking therapy for childhood wounding—being bullied as a kid, suffering the pain of racism. He went to Jerusalem and visited the Wailing Wall but found that even there, people knew of him and his fall from grace. Slowly, opportunities showed up—becoming a senior fellow at the Center for American Progress and teaching at Princeton. By 2011, he was rising, launching the Rebuild the Dream campaign (now called the Dream Corps), intended as a progressive counterpart to the Tea Party. In April 2012, he published his second book, titled *Rebuild the Dream*. It debuted at number 16 on the *New York Times* bestsellers list.

The recovery was slow, but Van saw the seeds of the breakthrough, and he watered them. He described his process to me:

> *A breakdown hurts, but there is always a gift in the wound, a blessing in the curse. After a fall that hard, you know what it's like to be on the bottom. You have empathy for other folks who've lost out as well—white guys in red states in the rust belt who used to have good jobs and a good town, but now the factory is gone, the job is gone. They're hurt, and they lash out and make bad choices. What I went through humanized me. I've had enough success and enough failure that I can relate to the impermanence of both. My failure gave me an independence of spirit so I don't have to always defend Democrats or do what other liberals are telling me to do. I had to find in myself my own source of peace and meaning, my own community, my own way.*

Through his public visibility as a popular political contributor on CNN, his success in getting the First Step Act into law, and the organizations he has founded to address issues of racism and inequality, Van's star has continued to rise. His honesty, humanity, and humor have made him one of our nation's most compassionate and compelling social commentators. Although he is a progressive activist, he is not bound by any ideology. His mission is to challenge people on the left and the right to stand in each other's shoes, to disagree constructively, and to bring the country together. Even after receiving the Jeff Bezos Courage and Civility award of $100 million in 2021, Van remains humble and focused on the stand of his committed life.

SEEKING A PLANETARY
BREAKTHROUGH

It is challenging enough to deal with our own personal break-downs, but we humans are faced with an epic planetary break-down: global warming and climate change. We have other crises as well: the pandemic and the retreat from democracy through-out the world. But the climate crisis is different in that it has a time limit. We have to take radical action within the next 10 years in order to avert further societal collapse.

Earlier, I presented Paul Hawken's view that global warming is happening for us rather than to us. I assert that even though the disasters are coming harder and faster than ever before, that is still true—our current planetary breakdown offers the seeds of the greatest breakthroughs that we've ever seen. The story underneath the story is the epic beginning of a massive trans-formation of the human condition. The breakdowns are so vast that they're bringing us together. We are realizing that we are one biology, that we are one human family that can have a col-lective breakthrough. Imagine the impact of many millions of people choosing to commit themselves to the kind of systemic change that will bring about a breakthrough for humanity!

CHAPTER 9

From Scarcity to Sufficiency

Gratitude creates a sense of abundance, the knowing that you have what you need. In that climate of sufficiency, the hunger for more abates, and we take only what we need, in respect for the generosity of the giver.
—ROBIN WALL KIMMERER

When seeking to live a life of commitment, the mindset of scarcity can become our greatest challenge: "I don't know enough; there's not enough time or resources or support. I can't do this work and devote myself to my family . . ." It is a mindset that is debilitating but also transformable. I have seen the radical truth that *there is enough.*

You have read in chapter 1 the story of how my beloved mentor Buckminster Fuller laid the groundwork for my committed life. His talk that day in 1976 about the fact that the world has enough for all of humanity to thrive transformed my worldview and launched me into action. Bucky's scientific research had revealed to him the true capacities of our Earth to support all of humanity. Developed properly, used wisely, and distributed fairly, the Earth's bounties could enable everyone to have a high standard of living. What was holding us back was an unconscious belief that there is not enough.

Bucky also declared that the direction of humanity was to continue to innovate by doing more with less, so that even with a growing population, there would be enough for everyone everywhere to live a healthy and productive life. He spoke of this sufficiency not as an amount of anything, but rather as a state of being—a basic understanding of the integrity of the universe. I now had the distinctions of scarcity and sufficiency, and I began to see the world through the lens of enoughness. And that's when I started to see the sufficiency of everything and everyone.

My commitment to this paradigm began with The Hunger Project, whose original title was actually The End of Hunger: A Context of Responsibility and Sufficiency. That name didn't last, because people did not understand sufficiency, but I did. I began to live it, to teach it, and to raise millions of dollars based on it.

FUNDRAISING FROM THE HEART

My approach to fundraising for The Hunger Project was unique. You may recall from my introduction how Werner Erhard distinguished what he called the "two sides of the hand of hunger." One side is starvation and malnutrition, experienced at that time by a quarter of humanity, and the other side is the hunger for meaning, the hunger of people who have enough to eat but who crave to make a difference with their lives. It is this hunger that is rampant in the wealthier world. These two sides came together in The Hunger Project.

We understood that when people are in touch with their own sufficiency, they want to contribute. In my listening to people, I reflected back to them their own wholeness and enoughness, as well as the paradigm of a *you and me* world. In our conversations, they began to see it as a privilege to share what they had—especially with people living in conditions of hunger and poverty—and to be able to use their money to make a difference, to leave the planet better than they found it. This approach to fundraising was highly successful and led me to share it in a program for nonprofits called Fundraising from the Heart.

After 25 years of living and promoting this new paradigm, I wrote my first book, *The Soul of Money*, about the power of living your life from a context of Enough. Published in 2003 with a revised version issued in 2017, the book had a profound impact on hundreds of thousands of readers around the world. The Soul of Money Institute, which I run with my partner, Sara Vetter, is dedicated to helping people live a life of sufficiency, generosity, and fulfillment.

THE LIE OF SCARCITY

If you have read *The Soul of Money*, you may recall the basics of our approach to understanding scarcity and sufficiency. The Great Lie that we are all subject to is the mindset of scarcity: it's an unconscious, unexamined belief system that we all swim in but can rarely recognize, so pervasive is its grasp on our collective consciousness. We instinctively feel that the world is a place where there is just not enough to go around—that someone somewhere is always going to be left out, that more of anything and everything is better, and that's just the way it is.

I am not saying that scarcity does not exist. As someone who has worked directly with people in abject poverty, I am well aware that in too many places in the world (including the United States) there is not enough food, or clean water, or health care. I am not talking about people who are truly oppressed and marginalized, lacking the basics, including homes, jobs, and opportunity. I am speaking to a disease of the rest of us, the comfortable and relatively affluent, who fail to recognize that we actually have adequate resources for our lives and yet are driven by the desire for more. It is this scarcity mindset that I am addressing here, and it is what exacerbates hunger and poverty in the world, driving our global economic inequality.

I lived this unconscious assumption of scarcity for the first 30 years of my life, culminating in a lifestyle dedicated to acquiring more and better. As I mentioned earlier, Bill and I were entranced by the siren song of success. His work had the money flowing, and I was devoted to spending it. We bought a big house in the best part of San Francisco and furnished it with fine art. We bought expensive new cars and clothes, took exotic vacations, and tried to be wine connoisseurs, in an attempt to keep up with our classy friends. Although we were loving parents, we didn't really question the fact that our kids were mostly cared for by the nanny and babysitters. In those days, I wasn't just focused on having more money and stuff; I felt insecure in many ways, worried about my weight, my clothes, whether people liked me or not, whether Bill would come back from a business trip. Scarcity had seeped into me and infected my soul.

It wasn't until I became steeped in The Hunger Project that we began to question our lifestyle and make changes to align it with the values of sufficiency and a commitment to service. After diving deeply into the work of personal and social transformation, Bill and I embraced a life of making a difference with our money and our lives. We expanded our relationships beyond the people we had mostly associated with and allocated our money toward projects and organizations devoted to things we cared about, like hunger, education, and ending poverty and abuse. We opened our large home to many, many guests who needed a place to stay. No longer trapped in my insecurities and fears, I was buoyed by a new sense of meaning in my life. I came to see that a new relationship with money was a portal to the vision of a world that works for everyone.

THREE TOXIC MYTHS OF SCARCITY

My work for the past four decades has been to illuminate how people of privilege must move from scarcity to sufficiency in our lives and in the world—beginning with recognizing the three toxic myths that hold the mindset of scarcity in place.

The first myth is that *there's not enough*—that there are too many people and not enough resources, food, water, money to go around. So, we have to compete and fight with each other to take care of our own. Someone somewhere is going to be left out, and we don't want it to be us or our families. If you really believe that, consciously or unconsciously, you feel obligated to make sure that you and yours will never be left out, which creates a separateness—an *us* and a *them*. It creates people hoarding and accumulating way more than they need. It legitimizes that and makes it responsible or even noble. We think rich people are cool—and we aspire to join their ranks.

The second toxic scarcity myth is *more is better*. More of anything and everything is better. We "need" more money, more square feet in our house, more furnishings, more cars, more

clothes and shoes, more toys, more vacations, more . . . more
. . . more. This is what drives our consumerist culture and the
destruction of our natural environment as we cut the trees, burn
the coal and oil, and pollute land and water to make ever more
stuff and "pave paradise to put up a parking lot." In a more
is better world, we overlook the obscene inequities that allow
the top 1 percent of people to own 43 percent of the world's
resources. We readily accept that it is okay for there to be a
growing number of millionaires and billionaires while one billion people live on less than $1 a day, and half of the world lives
on less than $10 a day.

Our need to possess more and more also drives much of the
violence, war, corruption, and exploitation of the planet. Nations
compete for more military might, more oil, more money, more
power. Corporations compete for more market share and more
profits, regardless of environmental and social impacts.

More is better is a race that has no end and no winners, an
addiction that never satisfies. In this mindset, even too much
is not enough. Millionaires and billionaires evade paying even
minimal taxes to support societal needs; their own net worth
is more important. And all of us, no matter what our financial
situation, are driven by the chase of more is better, even though
we rarely experience any payoff. The pursuit of more distracts
us from feeling satisfied with what we already have. It saps our
energy and our feelings of fulfillment. And sadly, we end up
defining our self-worth by our financial worth. When someone
asks if your children are successful, they aren't asking if they are
happy, they are really asking, "Are they making money?"

The third toxic myth is *that's just the way it is.* There is no
other way; this is the way it's always been and always will be.
This is the mantra we apply to everything we feel we have no

control over, no power to change. Resignation makes us feel helpless and hopeless and breeds cynicism. You just give up and succumb to playing the win/lose game.

ESCAPING THE TRAP OF MORE

My book *The Soul of Money* spoke powerfully to people who were caught in this game and realized they wanted out. Over the years, I've heard from thousands of people who broke the spell and transformed their lives. One of them is Sam Polk, who told his story in a memoir, *For the Love of Money: A Memoir of Family, Addiction, and a Wall Street Trader's Journey to Redefine Success.*

Sam came to Wall Street in his early 20s and by the age of 30 had become a senior trader in a huge hedge fund. Even during the 2008 market crash, he had made tons of money selling risky derivatives. When the firm offered him an annual bonus of $3.6 million, he found himself angry that it wasn't enough, and he demanded $8 million. His boss said he could get it if he stayed another seven years, but Sam realized he couldn't do it. He saw that he had lost himself in what he recognized was an addiction to more and more and more. His personal life was in a shambles, and he didn't like the man he had become. Making money was covering over a life of addiction and self-destructive behaviors. He realized that not only did he have enough, but he had more than he could possibly need.

In 2010, he quit Wall Street and moved to Los Angeles, determined to make a difference with his life. After a year or so of withdrawal and therapy that helped him confront and heal his sense of inadequacy, Sam got engaged in giving back. He spoke in schools and treatment programs. He created Groceryships, an organization that provides low-income families with money to buy whole, plant-based foods and learn about nutrition, cooking, and shopping, which has evolved into Everytable, a mission-driven food company that fights for food justice by making fresh, delicious food accessible and affordable for all. Sam now lives a committed life, a life of purpose, meaning, sufficiency, and fulfillment. He is happier than he's ever been.

THE PORTAL TO TRUE ABUNDANCE

The ground of being of a committed life is a sense of your own sufficiency. Gandhi said, "There is enough for our need, but not for our greed." It's important to make a very clear distinction between sufficiency and abundance. Sufficiency is not an amount of anything. It's not halfway between more than you need and less than you need. It's an experience of being met by the universe with exactly what you need. We all want abundance, or we think we do, but we are craving it from the mindset of scarcity—from fear and a need for protection in a not-enough world. But that kind of abundance easily turns into greed, excess, and waste. We accumulate way more than we need. In the name of false abundance, we overflow landfills, destroy ecosystems, and trash the oceans.

True abundance does exist, and it flows through the portal of sufficiency—the recognition of the beauty and wholeness of enough. The source of true abundance is not more, and it's not striving. You contribute not from a sense of lack, trying to fill up an emptiness in yourself, but rather from your experience of being complete and fulfilled. Our scarcity-based consumer culture has most of us living in an experience of deficit—feeling that there's something wrong with us and we need to acquire what we are lacking. In our obsessive pursuit of more, we race right past enough without even knowing what happened.

When I got in touch with my own sufficiency, I moved out of a deficit relationship with myself. It's not that I never have doubts about myself or that I never long for more of this or that or less of this or that. That still occurs, but it doesn't possess me the way it once did. The pettiness, the egoic concerns, are still available, and I still entertain them—I dance with them—but for the most part they don't get in my way. If I think I'm not okay, then I've got to fix myself. But if I realize that I am enough just the way I am, then I am free to focus on making a difference with my life.

WHAT YOU APPRECIATE APPRECIATES

You experience true abundance by going through the portal of sufficiency—by being grateful for what you already have. If you let go of trying to get more of what you don't really need—which is what we're brainwashed to do in this consumer culture—it frees up oceans of energy to pay attention to what you do have. When you are grateful for what you already have, it *expands*. This is the principle of sufficiency: What you appreciate appreciates.

I gained a new understanding of appreciation and contribution from Brother David Steindl-Rast, an extraordinary human being who personifies gratitude. Now in his late 90s, Brother David is a Benedictine monk who has no possessions and alternates between living in silent retreat and writing and teaching about gratitude as a way of life. If you don't know of him, I urge you to make his acquaintance at *gratefulness.org*. He is truly one of the great spiritual teachers of our age.

After reading *The Soul of Money*, Brother David graced me with a visit to my home, and our conversation about the "great fullness of life" moved me deeply. It is a state of grace and fulfillment that is available to us at all times. Gratitude is a place to live, a home. If you can find something to be grateful for, you can transform any situation. He says, "It is not happiness that makes us grateful, it is gratitude that makes us happy."

"When the bowl of life begins to overflow," Brother David says, "all you want to do is give, serve, and share." I have seen this kind of generosity throughout my decades as a fundraiser— from people at all levels of financial resources. The experience of sufficiency and fulfillment becomes accessible when they choose to make a difference with their money. When people use their resources to express their highest ideals and deepest values, their experience of their own wealth expands.

True wealth comes not from accumulating what we think we want, but from knowing we are blessed with what we truly need. When we are in touch with our sufficiency, our needs are met. My favorite poem from Sufi teacher Hazrat Inayat Khan expresses this perspective:

> *I asked for strength*
> *and God gave me difficulties to make me strong.*
> *I asked for wisdom*
> *and God gave me problems to learn to solve.*
> *I asked for prosperity*
> *and God gave me a brain and brawn to work.*
> *I asked for courage*
> *and God gave me dangers to overcome.*

I asked for love
and God gave me people to help.
I asked for favours
and God gave me opportunities.
I received nothing I wanted.
I received everything I needed.

PART III

Challenges, Change, and Completion

Awareness of the challenges you face enables you to navigate them, finding within yourself capacities that you may not know you have or that you may need to develop.

CHAPTER 10

Being Tested

The best moments usually occur when a person's body or mind is stretched to its limits in a voluntary effort to accomplish something difficult and worthwhile.
—MIHALY CSIKSZENTMIHALYI

If you make a commitment larger than your own life—a commitment that is beyond what you know you're capable of—you will, for sure, be tested. And if that commitment is in service of life, you will pass those tests because it's not about you. If it were about you, then you would give up and try something else. When it's not about you, the commitment reshapes you into someone who can meet and prevail in that test. It's in the process of delivering the desired result that you gain the skills you need, that you are forged into the person you need to be. When I committed to ending hunger, I had no idea how to do it. Yet I learned how to inspire people and get them involved, generate and manage teams of volunteers, raise huge sums of money, and interact with anyone in the halls of power or in a dusty refugee camp.

Being tested is how we learn—it is how I learned. This chapter illuminates some of the ways my commitment was challenged: by competing commitments, by overwhelm and overcommitment, by illnesses, and by temptation to take on what was not mine to do. Your tests will be different than mine, but as you face them, I hope these stories will bolster your commitment and your confidence.

COMPETING COMMITMENTS

In living a committed life, a primary test for me—and especially for women everywhere—is competing commitments. It is primarily the commitment of motherhood that is unequivocal, not something you can suddenly say about it, "Oh, I didn't mean that. Sorry, I can't do that now. This is just too hard . . ." Men, of course, face managing both career and family, but since homemaking and child-rearing remain the primary domain of women, mothers are often more greatly challenged.

In 1977, when The Hunger Project started, I was 32 years old and my kids were three, five, and seven. At first I was just going to help out for a few months, but soon it swept me off my feet. I was completely devoted to my children, and I was also completely devoted to ending hunger. Within a few years, I was managing tens of thousands of Hunger Project volunteers and running fundraising operations in countries throughout the world. I was traveling constantly. Bill was a steadfast dad, great with the kids, and we had a wonderful nanny named Tuti who lived with us, but I felt a lot of guilt and struggle.

Wherever I was, I wasn't really there. In a meeting at the UN, or being in Ethiopia, or raising money in Japan, or wherever I was, I would think, "Oh my god, it's my day to bring snacks to Billy's class. Oh no, I forgot to tell the nanny . . ." Or I would try to get back for my daughter Summer's Spring Sing, and I would miss a plane in New York, or some connection wouldn't be made, and I wouldn't get back to Zack's ball game. I was torn, ripped apart, certain that I was screwing up my children forever. All that happened again and again, as you can well imagine if you're a working mom. Even though what I was doing was so important to me, I felt guilty about it. I'd been raised a Catholic, and guilt was my middle name. I became a walking apology to my children and often to Bill, thinking that apology, like confession, could absolve my sins.

After about three years of this tortuous juggling, I called a family meeting. The kids were about 6, 8, and 10. We all sat on the floor in a circle around a coffee table in our family room. Speaking through my tears. I told my family, "I only meant to help out with The Hunger Project for a little while, but now I've become committed to ending world hunger. I want you to know that I'm really doing it for you kids. I want you to live in a different world. I'm so sorry I'm not here. I'm sorry I've missed so many key events in your lives. I'm doing the best I can, and I know I'm going to continue this work to end hunger. I need your permission. I need your blessing."

My daughter, Summer, who was eight, said, "Mom, if you can end world hunger, you don't have to take us to the orthodontist. Someone else can do that." At that, we all started laughing and crying.

Then my son Basil said, "Mom, we have the coolest life. We've got people from Africa staying in the guest room. We've got people from the UN at breakfast. We can take all these amazing things to school for show and tell. When other kids are going to Disneyland for spring break, we go to Micronesia. We love our life. We're so proud of you."

We were all hugging and crying, and then my youngest one, Zack, said how he loved that he brought a mask from Zambia to show to his first-grade class. It was such a hit. All three kids and my husband Bill just overwhelmed me with their permission, their gratitude, their blessing, saying, "Sometimes it's sad that you miss things, but we love you and we're proud of you and your work. Plus, we have the coolest life!"

It was after this meeting that Bill became involved as a financial adviser to The Hunger Project and eventually chaired the US board. My children came to the office after school and volunteered, stuffing envelopes, organizing the mail, and sitting under my desk doing their homework. The Hunger Project became a family affair.

This miraculous meeting didn't end my guilt completely or my regrets about missing a lot of my children's lives, but it buoyed me. And I came to know the profound truth of the saying, "It takes a village to raise a child." Our family came to rely on a wide support system of friends, relatives, teachers, neighbors, and coaches. I called on other parents and mentors, who not only provided a shoulder to cry on but also mirrored me to myself, confirming that my commitment was for my family as well as for the world and that I was modeling for my children a life of service.

Over the years, I have made relative peace with my lack of presence with the kids, as I have seen that it also had its gifts.

They became more independent and relied on each other more and on their father, strengthening those bonds. They had relationships with extraordinary people like Jane Goodall and Bucky Fuller. John Denver sang in our living room. People from all over the world lived with us for weeks or months, exposing them to cultures, food, and fun that most people only dream of experiencing. Perhaps all these assets balanced out the liabilities of not having Mom around. My children have indeed thrived and engaged in meaningful work in the world.

I don't make light of the challenge, however, of competing and conflicting commitments where parents don't have the resources for nannies and babysitters. Yet mothers have done it since time immemorial. I am especially blown away by and bow to the single mothers of today. The magnitude of all that they carry alone every day is stunning and inspiring. It is an expression of how extraordinary today's women are that as they continue to rise in leadership in the workplace and in transforming society, they find the strength and courage to discover ways to balance meaning and purpose with nurturing children and maintaining family life.

OVERCOMMITMENT AND OVERWHELM

Overcommitment and overwhelm are kind of a daily experience for me, though I would say that I have a constantly growing capacity from having dealt with it my entire life. It began in kindergarten. I was our teacher Miss Edna's star student, tutoring other kids in reading, and I organized our class to have lemonade and chocolate chip cookie stands after school to raise money for the sixth-grade play. I had too much to do when I was five years old, and I'm still a sucker for that. The depth of my passion and the breadth of my relationships mean I have a very difficult time saying no. I spent many years complaining about it; whining to friends, coworkers, and coaches; even crying like I was the victim of some horrible Greek tragedy.

My counselors would inevitably sit me down and say, "Let's look at all the things on your plate." And we'd make lists and charts and piles on the floor, and they'd say, "You don't need to do that; you can delegate that to this person." Or "Do you really need to do that now?" I began to see that when I'm scattered and trying to do too many things at the same time and doing things incompletely, I'm overwhelmed. And I learned that the antidote is to focus on one thing and to do it completely. When I can do that, it seems to move everything else forward. So, I've learned to respect my overcommitment tendency and not resist it. The integrity of completion frees me and creates some space.

NOT MINE TO DO . . .

Because living my commitments has shaped me into an effective human being, I've stepped into arenas that aren't mine. It happens often in my daily life—like when our family is out to dinner and someone didn't get what they ordered, I jump in and call the waitperson for them. I've often gotten hooked and caught by trying to tap into something that's actually not mine to do. When the Pachamama Alliance went through a challenging shift from a hierarchical organization to what's called a flat or distributed leadership organization, I wanted to jump in to help make things work, but I realized that I am not an organizational development consultant—that's not my swim lane.

Sometimes I can hardly stand to stand by, but I learned a powerful lesson about what is mine to do from one of the Nobel

Peace Prize winners, Máiread Maguire. In 1976, along with Betty Williams, she had organized thousands of women and mothers in peaceful protests that led to the end of the bitter conflict between Catholics and Protestants in Northern Ireland. In 2013, I accompanied Máiread and other members of the Nobel Women's Initiative—Leymah Gbowee, Jody Williams, and Shirin Ebadi—as well as some financial supporters on a trip to Liberia.

One afternoon, we went with Máiread to see the conditions of a women's prison in Monrovia. The prison was a small run-down building with a dirt courtyard in the middle. There were six or seven cells of different sizes holding five or six women of all ages. In one, a teenage girl nursed her baby. We wandered through, stopping to talk to them through the bars, as the people in Liberia speak English.

"How long have you been here?"—"I don't know."

"How did you get arrested?"—"They came and got me."

"What's your crime? What are you being accused of?"—"I don't know."

"Have you been to trial?"—"No."

"How long will you be here? Do you have a sentence?"—"No."

"Do you have children?"—"Yes, I have five children."

"Who is caring for them?"—"I don't know."

They were so in the dark, and it was heartbreaking. The cells were barren, with only cots on the dirt floors—no television, no reading material, even though some of the women knew how to read. We learned their names; we touched their hands through the bars. I came away determined that we had to get them out of that prison. This wasn't the purpose of our trip—we had a whole other agenda—but back at our hotel, I couldn't stop thinking about the prisoners. I was obsessed, almost panicked, pacing the lobby crying and thinking about what to do. Máiread, an angel of a woman, all kindness and compassion, saw how agitated I was and sat down with me. She took me in her arms as I cried, and I said, "Máiread, we can't leave them there. We've got influence. We've got to get them out of there."

Máiread took my hands in hers, looked me in the eyes, and said, "Lynne, you can't do everything. You need to determine what's yours to do. Then know that other people will take care of the things that aren't yours to do. You need to take care of your source, your heart, your soul, because if you don't, you won't be able to give anymore. This is not what we're here for— and not what your job is. You need to let go of this one. We can make a contribution to them, but saving them is not your work."

After many tears, I let it go. I knew she was right. Then followed a small miracle. At that moment, an American friend who is married to a Liberian found us in the lobby and said, "I just got a bunch of books and magazines from the States that I want to give to people in Liberia." Sure enough, they arrived in the lobby, and we went through them, picking out what we thought would be appropriate for the incarcerated women. The next day, we went back to the prison and delivered the books and magazines, spending some time reading from them and showing them pictures. It was like food for them, and they were ecstatic. We brought along a guitar and sang and danced in the courtyard. We left the guitar there: now they had books and music; they had things to do.

The next day, our group met with the minister of justice and told her about the prison—that the women didn't even know why they were there, that there seemed to have been no trials and sentences. She listened intently, and I could see that she was disturbed, but it was clear that she was overwhelmed with the challenges to her government in this postwar period. We were not able to help get those women released from prison, but I do know that we at least made a contribution to their lives there. And I learned a lesson that would serve me my entire life: I can't do everything—focus on what is mine to do.

ILLNESS: CURSES AND HEALING

Some years ago, a national magazine called *Balance* contacted me about doing an interview. They wanted to put me on the cover as an example of a successful, busy woman maintaining balance in her life. I had to decline the interview because, as I told them, "I don't live a balanced life. I'm not committed to seeking balance in life. I'm an *all-in* person. I give my all to everything I do, which means I will sometimes work till I drop, or not exercise enough or sleep enough or eat right. I'm afraid I'm not a good model at all for your readers."

I had struggled with balance for a long time, but eventually I gave up on it. I realized that my commitment is to being in integrity, keeping my word, and getting a job done. I give myself permission to be true to myself, and often that requires giving my all. I'm not saying that is the right way to be and that balance is wrong, it's just what's true for me. And mostly it has worked in my life.

I am blessed to have a strong constitution and am dedicated to a healthy lifestyle; however, at times in my life I have ignored my physicality and been irresponsible about my own physical capacities. I have not given my body the respect it needs to support my commitments, my spirit, and my love for the world. So, over the years I have gotten sick, sometimes seriously, but my healing has always generated a needed breakthrough.

I have recounted how many months of dealing with what turned out to be malaria stopped me in my tracks at The Hunger Project. Getting sick was the breakdown that led to the breakthrough of creating the Pachamama Alliance with Bill and John Perkins. Years later, when we were living in Ecuador for a time, both Bill and I were struck with an unexplained illness for which there seemed to be no satisfactory medical diagnosis.

At this time, 2013, the government of Ecuador was trying to expand oil production, and the Indigenous organizations, including our affiliate Fundación Pachamama, were in the way. Our organization was a central hub of Indigenous efforts to prevent further oil extraction in their territories. Government operatives converged on Fundación Pachamama offices in Quito, made off with files and equipment, and shut us down. Director Belen Paez was frightened. She was being followed and her phone was tapped. Bill and I had just flown to New York for a fundraiser when we succumbed to what we thought was the flu, but both of us got sicker and sicker, and the doctors couldn't figure out what was the cause. Our colleague, the Sápara shaman Manari Ushigua, was also sick. He explained that shamans can use their powers to disrupt and injure if they choose to do so, and he believed that we had all been cursed by what he called dark shamans hired by the government to stop our work there.

Once our Ecuador operation was shut down, it was in complete disarray and could no longer receive grants. At the same time, the Pachamama Alliance in San Francisco was facing a financial crisis when we lost a donor who had pledged $1.5 million but came through with nothing. Our illness forced Bill and me back to the States to handle the financial health and well-being of the Pachamama Alliance. Several friends who are shamans themselves came to our home to heal us, smudging every inch of the house, cleansing us in ceremonies, and blocking the invisible "poison darts" they saw coming our way.

Bill began to recover, but I got sicker and sicker. My entire body seemed to be shutting down, and I felt like someone who was just fading away. There followed months of seeking healing. I connected with a wonderful Korean doctor, Dr. Choe, who took us to see some remarkable healers in Korea. It was an intense time, during which our Indigenous partners helped us see that the attack on our organization indicated how powerful our work was in Ecuador. We would not have been attacked if our alliance had not been making a significant difference. So we started to see the attack as a kind of badge of honor.

Somehow that realization gave me strength, and I began to heal. I left Korea for Japan, where I had an incredibly successful speaking and fundraising tour, which invigorated me further. Once again, I felt like my body had offered a lesson—and pulled me through into a new space. We reformulated Fundación Pachamama as a consulting firm and continued our work. In San Francisco, we re-sourced and reorganized the Pachamama Alliance, and by 2015 we were back on track, having the best years we'd ever had.

ILLNESS: FEEDBACK FROM MY HEART

In 2018, I had another health challenge that once again reshaped my approach to my commitments. I started experiencing a fluttering in my heart—different palpitations that were scary. You don't think about your heartbeat until it's out of rhythm and you can't sleep; you almost can't think. The treatment for this atrial fibrillation is called an ablation—not a surgery, but a procedure done laparoscopically to shut down the electrical impulses that are confusing the heart muscle.

I was blessed to have a remarkable doctor, Gigi Dunn, who aimed to have me be totally accountable for what was happening, beginning with helping me realize why my heart was in breakdown. She drew an image that I can't reproduce here, but imagine an hourglass that is sort of like a huge X. She pointed to the top part of the X and said, "This is your commitment to the world, and it is only going to grow. It's clear you are not going to stop working on transformation, on all the causes you care about, so I don't expect that."

Then she told me, "Everybody has different ways of being in the world. Some people work primarily through their gut. Some people work primarily through their mind. Some people work primarily through their voice. Some people do everything through the heart. That's your way of living and being and giving your contributions to the world." She drew this heart right in the center of the X and said, "All of this commitment above is going through your heart. We are not going to mess with this top triangle. We're going to work on this bottom triangle. To support the work that's going on above, this lower part needs to be just as big. Your commitment to your body, your self-care, needs to get bigger. You have to do that for your heart, because everything goes through your heart."

In a way, atrial fibrillation was a perfect illness for me. That diagram totally changed the way I was looking at taking care of myself. I did not need to diminish my commitment; rather, I needed to build my capacity in new ways. I was being called to take the same level of responsibility for my body that I'd taken for making the world work for everyone with no one and nothing left out. Again, my body seemed to be giving me some intense feedback—this time that it was no longer appropriate for me to be leading everything for everyone. I began to create more room for Sara Vetter and other colleagues at the Soul of Money Institute. I stepped back from being the primary fundraiser at the Pachamama Alliance and aimed at empowering staff people. This transformation came just in time for the new way of living demanded by COVID-19.

I don't recommend getting sick, but sometimes the body gives us intense feedback that we have to pay attention to. In every case when I've gotten ill, I've seen—not right away, of course, but eventually—the wisdom of my body, and I've accepted the teaching. My body would crash just at the right time to give me the feedback I needed to change the game. Getting sick is not a failure; it's our body letting us know that it's working for us— just like Mother Earth is now giving us the feedback we need to take an evolutionary leap for humankind.

CHAPTER II

Being Proximate to Suffering

When you get proximate to the excluded and the disfavored,
you learn things that you need to understand if we're going
to change the world. Our understanding of how we change
things comes in proximity to inequality, to injustice.
—BRYAN STEVENSON

In the early 1990s, I was in Calcutta for a Hunger Project meeting and heard that Mother Teresa was there also. In hopes of seeing her again and volunteering some time, I went to the Mother House, which was called Kaligaht. I met her just as she was leaving for the leprosy center, and I asked if I could go with her. I had only heard about leprosy in books and movies and knew it to be a horrendous disfiguring disease, but I felt compelled to go. It could not be worse, I thought, than what I had seen as a young woman volunteering in the children's burn unit in a Chicago hospital where I had played piano, sung songs, and visited with the kids, some of whom were burned beyond recognition. Accompanying Mother Teresa that day, I witnessed her giving physical affection to everyone she came in contact with—embracing bodies covered with sores, kissing a partially missing face, holding people's wrists if they had no hands. And though I had heard that leprosy was a contagious disease, I could not stop myself from reaching out physically as well. I was completely unafraid, feeling I was carried by her grace and her love for God.

I found myself in the presence of a man who had just been brought to the center, all skin and bones, almost a skeleton. He had been sleeping in the streets and had sores all over his body. He lay on a cot, and I sat next to him on a tiny stool. He could not speak, so I did not know his name but I told him mine, and then I took his hand and said I would like to sing to him. He was dying, but he was not struggling. He lay there peacefully and quietly while I sang—I don't know for how long—and I sang until he expired. At that point in my life, he was the first person I had been with at death, and I was profoundly moved.

After, Mother Teresa took my hands in hers and looked into my eyes. "You are an angel," she said. "You are an angel. You are an angel." She said it three times, as if to make sure it landed. And that is exactly what I felt—like I was somehow an insubstantial wisp, like you could put your hands right through me. Again, divine guidance had delivered me into a realm of unimaginable suffering and given me the greatest of gifts: a way to express my love.

Much later in life, I learned the phrase "getting proximate to suffering," but I realized that it is something I have been drawn to throughout my life. The phrase comes from Bryan Stevenson, a lawyer, a social justice activist, founder of the Equal Justice

Initiative, and author of the book *Just Mercy: A Story of Justice and Redemption*. His work to defend people who are wrongly incarcerated, to seek justice for underserved communities, and to raise consciousness about America's horrendous treatment of African Americans has made him one of my great heroes of commitment.

OPENING TO THE
PAIN OF THE WORLD

When you live a committed life, you become intolerant of injustice and unstoppable in addressing the things that you believe in. That stance is a huge blessing, but it's also a liability because you can't turn away from the suffering of the world. You feel the world's problems in your cells, in your blood, and in your body. In a *you and me* world, if you are suffering, I am suffering. Yet it is one thing to feel that connection and that responsibility and another thing to be up close and personal with the people who are suffering—to know their names, to sit with them, to touch them and to hear their stories.

I have previously mentioned Will Keepin's *Twelve Principles of Spiritual Leadership*, which have been a source of profound guidance for me. His ninth principle speaks directly to this subject:

> **The ninth principle is do not insulate yourself from the pain of the world.** We must allow our hearts to be broken—broken open—by the pain of the world. As that happens, as we let that pain in, we become the vehicles for transformation. If we block the pain, we are actually

preventing our own participation in the world's attempt to heal itself. As we allow our hearts to break open, the pain that comes is the medicine by which the Earth heals itself, and we become the agents of that healing. This is a vital principle that is quite alien to our usual Western ways of thinking.

With "Western ways," he is referring to our avoidance of suffering, which was true of me as well when I began my committed life. In the early years of The Hunger Project, my work had been in organizing and fundraising, primarily in the United States, Canada, and Europe, where I was spreading the message of the possibility of ending world hunger and amassing resources to fund our work of creating a new context of awareness and support. I didn't really get up close and personal with hunger until 1983, when I went to India. At this time, the country had not yet made great strides in overcoming hunger and poverty.

Just off the plane in Bombay, I was immediately accosted by the heat, foul odors, and a barrage of beggars, and soon I was immersed in the reality of people living in extreme poverty: families living in tents and makeshift huts in the airport parking lot, on the roads and streets, in doorways and alleys; women cooking on little metal cans of fire; people defecating in the street outside my hotel. I visited massive slums where 75,000 people shared one water spigot; and everywhere, children with pleading eyes held out their emaciated hands to me. By my third day in India, I was overwhelmed and in a kind of shock. I had talked about it a lot, but I had never experienced starving people and never seen massive malnutrition and poverty-related hunger. What is the way through here? What is a pathway from this horrendous, overwhelming experience?

Had I not made the commitment to end world hunger—and made it so publicly—I would have just said to myself, "This is hopeless. Who are you kidding? What kind of an arrogant person would think that they could do something about this? This is way over your head." But my commitment was stronger than the confrontation. I was so deeply surrendered to it, so completely dedicated to it with my whole body and soul, I knew I could never turn away from it. No matter what the circumstances, I was a stand for the end of hunger, and it was that commitment that pulled me through.

This was true of everyone I worked with: especially our Indian colleagues, who were some of the most extraordinary leaders I've ever known. Our commitment was so deep and fierce within us that we couldn't resign ourselves to hopelessness. We couldn't go there. We had to prevail. And in prevailing, we were shaped, molded, and forged into who we needed to be to keep going, no matter what. We let go of caring what people thought of us, whether they thought we were silly or naive, and we focused on what Martin Luther King Jr. said about "making a way out of no way."

CONFRONTING THE
LEGACY OF RACISM

Most recently, I have engaged with the thousands and thousands of Black Americans who are remembered and honored at the Legacy Museum and the National Memorial for Peace and Justice in Montgomery, Alabama. This sacred place, which I visited in 2019, is the creation of Bryan Stevenson's Equal Justice Initiative and commemorates the experience of African Americans, as emblazoned on the building, "From Enslavement to Mass

Incarceration." I've heard it called "the lynching memorial," for the installation features the names and dates of the public torture and murder of men, women, children, and families whose only crime was the color of their skin. Lynchings and burnings, it seems, were a form of public entertainment in the South—10,000 spectators watched a 15-year-old boy hanged for drinking from a white man's well. A 16-year-old boy was burned alive in a public spectacle lynching before thousands in Polk County, Florida, in 1901. David Walker, his wife, and their four children were lynched in Hickman, Kentucky, in 1908 after Mr. Walker was accused of using inappropriate language with a white woman.

Bryan Stevenson's stand to have Americans honestly confront racism and the legacy of slavery, lynching, and segregation opened me to a new realm of being proximate to suffering. I was stunned that I did not know the full extent of this history—that I had not yet gone toward the suffering of Black Americans in the way I had with marginalized women in India and victims of violence in Africa. I had witnessed truth and reconciliation processes in Liberia and South Africa, but not here in my own country.

Bryan has said, "Our nation's history of racial injustice casts a shadow across the American landscape. This shadow cannot be lifted until we shine the light of truth on the destructive violence that shaped our nation, traumatized people of color, and compromised our commitment to the rule of law and to equal justice." He references Germany, where the Nazi death camps of Treblinka and Buchenwald and Auschwitz have been preserved for people to visit and learn from. In cities and even in the small towns, there are monuments to the Holocaust with the admonishment "Never forget." Yet here in this country, rather than confess, we have done our best to cover over the history of American genocide.

Getting proximate to suffering is a test that all of us need to confront, and those of us who profess to live committed lives are most challenged to open and deepen our hearts. My friend the Reverend Deborah Johnson says, "You can't heal what you can't feel." If we can't feel, physically and emotionally, the pain of those we seek to partner with and support—if it's just intellectual, if it's just statistics and nameless figures in a newscast—we can't ultimately be truly, authentically useful.

SARA'S STORY: WITNESSING
THE HEART OF DARKNESS

In my work with the Nobel Women's Initiative, I was called on to bear witness to unimaginable atrocities. In our work to amplify the voices of women in seeking an end to war and violence, I was present at a number of gatherings where women recounted their horrific stories of enduring rape, torture, and the brutal murder of their loved ones. I knew their names; I have held them as we cried together.

One dramatic story about the Nobels is not mine but is the story of my most treasured ally, friend, and partner in the Soul of Money Institute, Sara Vetter. It may help to know a bit about Sara, a remarkable woman who transformed her life after connecting with the Pachamama Alliance and the Soul of Money Institute. Sara is blessed with great beauty, charm, and charisma. But underneath her stunning exterior is a depth of soulfulness and a capacity for compassion and commitment, as well as a refreshingly awesome and sometimes irreverent sense of humor. I could not have a more exquisite partner!

Sara grew up in a wealthy but dysfunctional family. She married a man who became very successful as one of the early executives of Microsoft Corporation. They had three children and lived a life of supreme privilege among the wealthy elite, which included Bill Gates, Warren Buffett, and others. But a happy marriage and a contented life was something their money could not buy. Divorced in her early 40s, Sara was adrift and miserable and began seeking a more spiritual path. We met at a Silicon Valley fundraiser and had a powerful connection. Soon she was partnering with me in fundraising for the Pachamama Alliance, traveling with us to the Amazon, participating in our Soul of Money programs, and discovering what was to become her committed life.

In 2013, when I was laid low by the dark shamans in Ecuador and too sick to travel, Sara took my place on a journey arranged by Nobel Prize laureate Leymah Gbowee to the Democratic Republic of Congo (DRC). The trip was part of the Nobel Women's Initiative campaign to stop gender violence and rape in war-torn areas. The DRC was the heart of darkness in terms of the treatment of women, where it was said that every day, dozens of women were raped and violated. The Nobels' delegation came to bear witness to these atrocities and to offer support to the victims.

It turned out that the delegation was only three women: Leymah, an extraordinary force of nature; a donor philanthropist named Hillary; and Sara. The guts and courage it took for her to take my place was quite incredible. Here is Sara's remarkable story as she told me:

> *The three of us, each with a bodyguard, traveled to Bunia, where grassroots activists were doing workshops for women survivors of rape and sexual violence. Women had traveled for days on foot to be there and had been together for a*

couple of days when we arrived to be of support to the process. They were so excited to see Leymah—I'm not sure what they thought of these two white women accompanying her. There were about 25 women of all ages (it was hard to tell anyone's age), some of whom were holding babies.

Leymah Gbowee conducted a process for the women to share about their experience and to be held and heard by their sisters sitting around the table. She said, "Okay, who would like to share their story?" No one lifted a hand. Finally, one woman raised her hand and started to tell her excruciating story. For a woman of my background, it was something I had never heard even on a TV show. She said it so clearly, describing how she had been tied to a tree, raped by 10 different soldiers who left her for dead. She managed to return home but was completely disowned by her own family because now she was soiled property. She had nowhere to go but was eventually taken to a place of refuge and was able to somewhat heal herself.

There followed story after story, as each of the other women got the courage to speak. Each story was more gut-wrenching than the last one. Some of the women worked in the mines, where the male miners would rape them. Others were attacked by marauding soldiers. I recall the story of two girls, 13 or 14, who were each holding babies. They had been raped by a family member, and then their family had thrown them out. All the victims had nowhere to go until they were found by groups offering medical care and a place to heal.

During the day, Hillary and I were almost frozen. We almost couldn't speak or breathe. We were on the floor, barely holding ourselves up. I wanted to just curl up in a ball and sob, but I knew I couldn't. I kept thinking, "With what these women went through, who am I to even be here? Why am I even sitting in this room? What can I do? I don't even belong here."

Leymah, however, was composed and compassionate. When all the stories were told, she sat in silence for a moment and then spoke softly but firmly. She said, "I want to tell you something. This is really important. I want all of you to listen very carefully." They all kind of leaned in. Leymah called in the group facilitator and a volunteer and tied their hands together with a scarf. Then she instructed them to walk around the room. They sort of wobbled around very awkwardly.

Then she said, "See how you're chained to each other? Imagine that person, tied to you with that scarf, is your abuser, the person who's done the most horrific thing to you ever imaginable. Not that you'll ever forget him. You will probably never forget him, but you have to forgive him. Because if you don't forgive him, you will be chained to him for the rest of your life. You will never, ever, ever be free of the pain and the sorrow of what he's done to you and your family until you are able to actually forgive him. If you can't forgive, you will never be free of him, never be able to move on. This is the only way you're going to get through this moment."

Almost instantly, the room lit up. To me it was almost inconceivable that you could ever forgive someone who did something like that to you. But the women seemed to get it. They started sobbing and hugging each other. They came together and formed a circle, holding on to each other. Suddenly, the room was vibrating with joy and laughter. I could feel the complete relief in every woman in that room, and that blew me away.

Then they went out to the next room and started dancing. They went from sheer agony and pain to something like having a party. Joy, laughter, celebration, play came from inside them. It was possible because they had been heard, seen, loved, and supported. These women exuded more joy than the thousands of women I know who have all the luxuries in life. I will always remember the dancing. I will never forget that for the rest of my life.

On the last day of the trip, when I was still feeling like I had posttraumatic stress, we were interviewed by the press. The interviewer asked Leymah, "Why are you here? Why are you doing this? What good is it to be here and experience this? What are you going to bring back to the world?"

She said, "I'll tell you why I'm here. Every single one of these stories were the most atrocious stories I've ever heard, even in my own country—the most horrific things that I've ever seen happen to women in my life."

She drew with her finger a diagram of these circles of the rape, the abuse, the alienation, the struggle, all the horrible things, and then pointed to the middle. "In every single one of these stories, there was always a woman there and a beauty in the middle, helping other women to find some part of peace and freedom. No matter how horrific the circumstance, there's always a place of solidarity and sisterhood and the aliveness of the human spirit. To me, that's the strength that gets me through it. That's the strength that I want to bring back home and to the world: Every single time there was always a beauty in the middle."

THE BEAUTY IN THE MIDDLE

That phrase "Beauty in the Middle" became the theme for a photographic exhibition that was part of the United Nations Global Summit to End Sexual Violence in Conflict that Sara and I both attended in 2014. For the first time ever, 1,700 delegates from 123 countries listened to the stories of women ravaged by conflict. There, as in the Congo, it was clear what a huge difference being able to speak about suffering makes to both the speaker and those who listen. The experience of being in the DRC transformed my extraordinary partner, Sara, into one of the most powerful advocates for empowering women that I know.

It was also clear to me how such suffering galvanizes commitment. All of the women who were awarded the Nobel Peace Prize had suffered greatly. One of the original Nobels was Wangari Maathai, who was arrested and beaten up again and again as she struggled against poverty and injustice in her native Kenya. Máiread Maguire and Betty Williams witnessed the horrific violence of "the Troubles" in Northern Ireland. Máiread's sister's children were victims of a bomb attack. At age 12, Rigoberta Menchú Tum saw her entire family farm in Guatemala—people and animals—massacred before her eyes, and she was left for dead. Shirin Ebadi was the first woman judge in Iran, who, after the Islamic Revolution, was demoted to clerk; then she and her family were persecuted by the Iranian government for her legal work to defend women activists. Tawakkol Karman was a young woman leading the Arab Spring protests in Yemen. As with Shirin, her physical safety was threatened until she finally had to leave her country. Jody Williams, who led the campaign to end land mines, had suffered rape and other assaults in El Salvador.

All of these women turned their anguish and anger into an indomitable will to be of service to others who suffer. Endurance, stamina, and the will to live transformed their trauma into an unstoppable commitment to serve and bring peace to the world.

Knowing these women has humbled me and haunted me: I have never had to sacrifice to serve as they have. Yet I know that suffering knows no boundaries of privilege. It is so clearly taught in Buddhism that suffering is part of being human. It's not something you can ultimately avoid. It is part of the human condition. For some people, the suffering is so blatantly horrific that it's almost unbearable to even hear about it, but even for people of status and wealth, suffering has the same deep pain and scarring. The life that I've led has given me access to some of the wealthiest families on earth whose lives from the outside look glamorous but whose suffering in some cases is just as horrific and traumatic. Sometimes the abuse is even exacerbated by financial resources.

Being proximate to suffering may be one of the most difficult challenges of living a committed life, and it includes being present to your own suffering. Serving others is not meant to be an escape from the pain of your own life. Rather, service is an opportunity to transform your own hurt into growth and development, to deepen your own compassion. It requires you to open yourself up to what has been unacknowledged, stuffed away, and bring it into the light. To forgive ourselves is what allows us to heal, and healing ourselves allows us to serve and witness the healing of others.

CHAPTER 12

Loss, Failure, and Resilience

It is not the critic who counts. . . . The credit belongs to the man who is actually in the arena . . . if he fails, at least he fails while daring greatly.
—THEODORE (TEDDY) ROOSEVELT

In previous chapters, I've spoken to breakdowns, being tested, and witnessing suffering, and now I bring in loss and failure. It may sound like living a committed life is full of difficulties. But really, there are many joys to be had—as long as we are able to navigate through the losses and failures by learning to let go and by strengthening our determination and tapping into our resilience.

It may be useful to distinguish between loss—something taken away from us—and failure—something we may have created ourselves. Every human experiences loss, and in the end, each of us will lose everything. We all have what we think of as failures. Both loss and failure can be debilitating, or they can be generative, depending on our mindset and courage, a word derived from the French word coeur, which means "heart." What follows are some stories of people whose tenacity and resilience are remarkable, inspiring, and "en-couraging."

MY ADOPTED ANGEL DAUGHTER

I have three children by birth, Basil, Summer, and Zachary, and I also have an adopted "angel" daughter, Hafsat Abiola Costello. Hafsat, now in her 40s, is a brilliant and beautiful Nigerian woman who asked me to become her "angel" mother after her parents were both assassinated. She is an example of not only someone living a committed life but also someone who has had the courage to persevere through incredible loss. I met Hafsat in 1996 at the State of the World Forum, where I was a co-moderator, and she was part of the youth contingent. Tall, elegant, and eloquent, and also warm and humble, Hafsat was an imposing young woman about to graduate from Harvard. We bonded immediately.

In the 1990s, the Abiola family were the Kennedys of Nigeria. The patriarch, Moshood or MKO Abiola, had accumulated great wealth and entered politics to bring democratic change to the country then run by a corrupt and brutal military junta. Although he won the election for president in 1993 by a landslide, there was a military coup, and Abiola was arrested by the junta and charged with treason in 1994. He was imprisoned and allowed no visitors, not even family. His wife Kudirat Abiola fought mightily for his release, organizing marches and demonstrations and putting her own life in danger. Just days before she was to come to the United States for her daughter Hafsat's graduation from Harvard, Kudirat was murdered by the junta. After her assassination, Hafsat could not return to Nigeria. The family compound was destroyed, and her huge family was being hunted down. She was one of 18 children—her father's favored "angel child."

Remaining in the US, her family assets frozen, the 23-year-old Hafsat took responsibility for supporting her younger siblings while actively campaigning for international support for her father's freedom and her country's future. In honor of her mother, she began a foundation that continues still, the Kudirat Initiative for Nigerian Democracy, or KIND. In 1998, there was news that her father would be released, but a few days before his release was expected, he mysteriously died in prison, probably of poisoning. Devastated by the loss of both her parents, her family, and her life as she knew it, Hafsat turned to me for help and support, staying in our home and calling on me for strength and guidance.

Two years later, in 2000, when the junta was overthrown and Hafsat was finally able to go home, I received a call from her from Nigeria. She said, "I know I'm grown up, but I need a mother. Could you come and be my mother?" Surprised and honored, I flew to Lagos, where we gathered around her mother's grave in the family compound and had a beautiful ceremony that bonded us as spiritual mother and daughter. A year later, she brought her fiancé for a visit to make sure I approved of the marriage. I flew again to Lagos to officiate at their wedding, an event so popular that it was televised on Nigerian TV.

Over the past two decades, Hafsat has navigated her grief by devoting herself to her family and her work to foster democracy and uplift the status of women and girls. She lived in China, where she got her master's degree in international development (and learned Chinese!) and had two children. The family then moved to Brussels. She continues to run KIND, which works in Nigeria to provide women and girls with education and economic opportunities. She is also the president of the Women in Africa Initiative, the foremost platform working across all of Africa to help women entrepreneurs and leaders build successful businesses and strong economies.

The tragic circumstances of the murders of both of her parents could have crushed Hafsat, but she chose to live a committed life, bringing everything she received from her remarkable parents as well as her own talents and determination to serving her country and her continent. She sees her commitment not as a burden but a privilege—to carry on the work her parents died for. She continues to play a visible and courageous leadership role and has become one of the most respected and effective women leaders on the African continent.

FAILURE IS YOUR FRIEND

Who of us knows where our life is leading us and what challenges and losses may seem like failure? *Failure* is such a charged word. There is a sense of finality about it, like something has ended badly and one should perhaps be sad or ashamed. Yet actually, failure is simply feedback. You have committed to creating a result, and to achieve it you have taken whatever pathway was open to you or seemed most promising. If that pathway didn't work out, you try to figure out why and then move on to another pathway, and perhaps another. If you're committed, your failures are your most valuable feedback—your most formidable teachers and lessons. If you are open, every failure reveals something you did not see or understand. It gives you access not only to what you don't know, but also to what you don't know you don't know.

Abraham Lincoln ran for office and lost seven times before he became president. Orville and Wilbur Wright crashed quite a few planes before they finally flew. Elon Musk saw several SpaceX rockets blow up before a successful launch. He says, "If things are not failing, you are not innovative enough."

In 2010, the Pachamama Alliance was blessed to have a working relationship with the largest independent advertising agency in the country, Wieden+Kennedy, headquartered in Portland, Oregon. Visiting their offices, I was struck by a huge atrium in the center of the building. On one wall was a gigantic sign that said "FAIL HARDER." I thought, "What a weird motto for a company." But as I questioned founder Dan Wieden about it, he said, "We put everything into every idea, and then it flies or it doesn't. No matter what the job, we try everything and we fail, and then we might fail again and again until it flies. Our failures have given us our greatest insights."

NAVIGATING FUNDRAISING AND FAILURE

Sometimes, after you have failed and given up, something miraculous happens to resurrect your intention. In 1984, when the famine was raging in Ethiopia, The Hunger Project geared up to make a film about it to raise global awareness of the tragedy, and I managed to raise $500,000 from a generous donor. Just as we were in preproduction, the BBC came out with a powerful documentary that was shown worldwide and launched the Live Aid concert. At first, I remember thinking, "Oh my God, we failed. We didn't get there first." And we had to give the money back to the donor. Of course, the BBC, with a much larger budget, had done a better job than we could ever have done, but it was painful. We had hoped our film would establish

The Hunger Project as a major organization, but we just had to let it go. I had to remember the quote from Harry Truman, "It is amazing what you can accomplish if you do not care who gets the credit." Our intention had been to awaken the world to the tragedy in Ethiopia, and that intention was realized.

As a fundraiser for decades, I have had an interesting relationship with failure. When you are raising money, either it shows up or it doesn't—your results are crystal clear. When I first started fundraising for The Hunger Project, I formed the conviction that the money is always there—somewhere. If you cast a wide enough net and never ever give up, you will meet your goal. I began to find in myself a place where I was unstoppable. I closed off the idea that it was okay to make 80 percent of the target. I wouldn't even entertain the idea. That drove my husband Bill, who headed the US board of directors, and Dick Bishop, the chief financial officer at the time, completely crazy. As reasonable people, they wanted to plan for the worst-case scenario and be ready for it. But I just couldn't go there. They were trying to be fiscally responsible, and I refused to even participate in those conversations. We ended up having terrible arguments. Sometimes it was hard to get in bed with a man who would tell me 80 percent was good enough—someone who would plan on not meeting a target. It was like sleeping with the enemy! I'd tell him, "I can't take my energy and put it into what might go wrong, what might not happen. I just can't—you'll have to figure that out on your own."

It wasn't that I was afraid to fail. It was that my commitment to creating the end of hunger as an idea whose time had come was sacred to me. I was such a central player in The Hunger Project's culture to build and find the will to end hunger—which was what was missing—that I became an instrument of unyielding commitment. And to meet or exceed our financial targets, I had to be completely unreasonable. George Bernard Shaw said, "The reasonable man adapts himself to the world: the unreasonable one persists in trying to adapt the world to himself. Therefore, all progress depends on the unreasonable man." Or woman! For me, failure was not an option.

And, yes, I have had "failures" along the way—times when I made grave mistakes with serious financial consequences as well as losses that I had nothing to do with. I had cultivated a relationship with a very wealthy Japanese man who ended up donating millions of dollars to The Hunger Project. One year he gave a million dollars to purchase a farm in Zambia that was going to be a demonstration project. The government of Zambia was very corrupt at that time and the banking system was completely untrustworthy, so we put the transfer of the money in the hands of the chief justice of the Supreme Court there. That man just disappeared with the million dollars. We never found him or the money.

I was despondent, not only for the loss I had caused my friend—which was significant for him—but also because I started to feel hopeless about making any change in Africa. How could we help these people if every dollar that went toward Africa got in the wrong hands? How could we ever make a difference there? I realized I had to recover because I had to keep a network of 200,000 volunteers active and inspired. I was their folk hero, and I could not go down, I could not let them down. I found my way back to my own source of inspiration, which was my unyielding commitment. Recovery from failure is a key factor in living a committed life. The muscle of staying the course is what has gotten me through my doubts and fears and given me conviction and courage. It is an experience of profound integrity that is both freeing and fulfilling.

STEVEN DONZIGER:
COURAGE AND RESILIENCE

The antidote to what we call failure is fortitude, strength in facing adversity, and resilience, especially over a long period of time. A person who inspires me in this regard is my friend Steven Donziger, a man who I believe is a true human rights hero. As of this writing, his story has been 20 years in the making and has yet to reach a conclusion. It is a twisted legal saga that began in 1993 when Steven and other attorneys filed a class-action lawsuit in New York against the oil company Texaco on behalf of 30,000 Indigenous people in the Amazon rainforest. Massive contamination from Texaco's oil fields in the rainforest had polluted the land and water and poisoned many people, making them sick and shortening their lives.

In 2001, Chevron bought Texaco and took on the lawsuit and potential responsibility for cleaning up the damage and paying compensation. Chevron argued that the trial be transferred to Ecuador. In 2013, an Ecuadorean court ruled against the company and in favor of the Indigenous people and ordered it to pay $9.5 billion in damages. It was a stunning victory for the Indigenous Amazonian plaintiffs, but it was short-lived. Chevron refused to pay, moved the company's assets out of Ecuador, and threatened the plaintiffs with "a lifetime of litigation." Chevron found a corporate-friendly legal venue and judge in New York and put its energy into a countersuit, going after lead lawyer Steven Donziger, aiming to destroy him economically, professionally, and personally.

Through a series of legal maneuvers by Chevron, the judge eventually charged Steven with criminal contempt of court. The government prosecutor refused to take the case against him, and through an unusual arrangement, the judge arranged for him to be prosecuted by a private law firm, one with previous ties to Chevron. Awaiting trial, Steven was put under house arrest with a heavy ankle bracelet he had to wear day and night. He lost his law license and his ability to support his family, not to mention the potential tens of millions of dollars in legal fees. Through another legal maneuver, he was denied a jury trial, and in October 2021, the judge put him in a federal prison for six months. Because of COVID, he was released early in December 2021, but his house arrest continued until April 25, 2022, when he was finally set free. He had served 993 days on a petty charge for which the maximum sentence ever imposed on a lawyer was 90 days of home detention.

The Donziger case is a bizarre example of egregious injustice that is typical of totalitarian dictatorship. Chevron has spent an estimated $2 billion on lawyers, private investigators, and public relations consultants to harass Steven and has not paid a single cent to help the victims of pollution, lost farms, toxic water, cancer, and birth defects in Ecuador. Meanwhile, international lawyers, Nobel Prize laureates, the United Nations Human Rights Council, Amnesty International, Amazon Watch, Global Witness, Greenpeace, Canada's Assembly of First Nations, and the victims themselves continue to demand that Chevron pay the court-ordered judgment so that the Indigenous and farmer communities of Ecuador can heal their health crisis and restore their land and water.

You could say that Steven Donziger failed in his mission to hold Chevron accountable, but that is a shortsighted view.

His case has brought to light the collusion of parts of our legal system with private, monied interests. Despite severe sacrifices, Steven has remained doggedly determined to continue to seek justice for his clients. His courage and commitment are a beacon of light for human rights defenders around the world. If the arc of the moral universe does indeed bend toward justice, Steven will be exonerated, and Chevron will one day have to pay up.

GIVING OVER TO GUIDANCE

In Steven's case, dogged determination is called for, but sometimes courage, commitment, and resilience do not always demand that you persevere. Often, when things don't work, what gets revealed is that your goal may be honorable, but the pathway is flawed. Then it takes humility and the ability to let go—to let go of your ego, your old agenda, a strategy that isn't working. You can persevere in many ways, which may include stopping and starting over, taking the time to reexamine what went before and what may lie ahead. Making the distinction between giving up and giving over to guidance is a crucial one. You use your failure as feedback to reassess, reimagine, and redesign your next move. Letting go and letting yourself be guided by source, spirit, the universe, or your own version of guidance becomes the way forward. Some say, "Let go, let God." However it happens, it takes courage and resilience to follow the true callings of your commitment.

CHAPTER 13

Closure, Forgiveness, and New Openings

Nothing ever goes away until it has taught us what we need to know.

—PEMA CHÖDRÖN

There comes a time in a committed life when you feel it is time to complete an event or project and move on to what is next. Or perhaps completion is thrust upon you, and you find that you have to let go. Completion can occur whether or not you met your goal—it is about acknowledging and taking responsibility for what did and did not happen so that you can move forward. When we fail to complete things, it's hard to continue to create with integrity. A true completion generates an open space for new opportunities for the future. Endings can be joyous and easy or incredibly difficult and painful, and anywhere in between, and knowing how to navigate them takes insight and skill. That shows up in what is called *honorable*

163

closure, one of the great teachings from one of my mentors, anthropologist Angeles Arrien.

You can have an ending without closure: Something is over, but it haunts you. You think you have let go, but you find that you have unresolved feelings, disappointments, and regrets. Honorable closure is a process that allows you to free yourself from the past. You pay homage to what was brought into existence—the human effort, devotion, and dedication that it took. You assess the learning that occurred and forgive yourself and others for failures or transgressions. You can then stand on the shoulders of the accomplishment, and from there you can take new territory. Honorable closure generates a big open space where new opportunities start to show up with nothing lingering, nothing hanging over, nothing incomplete.

THE PROCESS OF
HONORABLE CLOSURE

My dear friend Linda Curtis is an executive coach and mindfulness teacher who specializes in honorable closure. She has practiced what she preaches, as she has had to find closure on the death of her beloved husband as well as with her parents, who shunned her when she left the Jehovah's Witnesses religion she was raised in. Endings, she says, are often poignant and sometimes painful, but it is actually innately human to want to end well, whether or not we know how to do it. To help people approach the process of ending something that is challenging or uncomfortable, she offers a four-step process for honorable closure. Each step has an associated quality.

The first step is to *tell the old story in a new way*, and the predominant quality of that step is gratitude. In the new telling, you look for what you are grateful for in that experience. Linda was certainly not grateful for her husband's death, but over the years she discovered a surprising number of unexpected outcomes that made her a better person and enriched her life—especially experiencing how much she was loved by others. When closure is necessary, she suggests mining the experience for new meaning and being grateful for what you learned and how you grew as a result.

Linda's second step is to *resolve any regrets that you may have with willingness and humility.* You may be in an ending because things didn't go right—you blew it somehow. You have to look in the mirror and acknowledge your own mistakes or misjudgments. How did I fail to show up in a way that might have improved the outcome? What behavior patterns are revealed that aren't working for me? It takes courage to tell the truth about your own shortcomings, but you don't have to beat yourself up. You resolve your regrets by owning them and learning from them.

The third step is to *let go of the past and let it be,* and the primary quality required is forgiveness—of yourself and others. You may not be ready to forgive yet, but you can have the aspiration to forgive at some point. And you can forgive yourself for not being ready to forgive yet. Anytime you're holding a grudge against another person, your energy is tied up and you are not free. The whole point of honorable closure is freeing up your energy and your spirit. Of her own experience Linda says, "Being shunned by my parents for leaving my religion was heartbreaking, and it took several years to forgive them and move forward, even as they continued to shun me. But I was committed to being happy and being free. Once I realized that forgiveness isn't about the past, it's about the present, I began to have a more spiritual perspective: that although the form of my relationship with them was different, you can't step outside of love. In their own imperfect way, they still loved me."

Linda's fourth step is to *invent the next story*, and that often is about reclaiming joy. When something ends, there's always something that's beginning. Now what? What do you see going forward? What is capturing your imagination and drawing you now? What kinds of future possibilities do you want to create and step into? You have to stop telling the old story and start a new one, and if you've done the closure work, you have more energy and attention to put toward the next new thing.

In Linda's experience, this four-step process is not necessarily linear. You can begin with any step. She says, "You don't just go, okay, I've made my list of what I'm grateful for. Check. I've resolved my regrets. Check. Oh yeah, I've forgiven him. Check. It doesn't work that way. Human beings are entitled to the dignity of their own process and timing."

For me, developing the skills of honorable closure is a hallmark of living a committed life. Some of the most powerful experiences of my life have been encounters with honorable closure, my own and among committed leaders I've been privileged to know. I've recounted how the ending of my work with The Hunger Project was so stressful that it took getting extremely ill with malaria to begin to let go of what I thought was a lifelong assignment. At the time, I felt like a victim of something, and it took me quite a while to see that it was actually an opportunity to transition gracefully to another chapter of my life. I could see that I was not a victim—that this was not happening to me, but happening for me. Honorable closure came when I saw that my fundamental stand for the end of hunger could take a different form through the Pachamama Alliance.

FORGIVENESS IS
LIFE CHANGING

When you think about honorable closure in your own life, you may find that the areas where you lack a sense of completion are experiences and relationships that require forgiveness—of yourself or others. When we hold on to resentments and grudges, negativity runs the show, and we are stuck in old beliefs, patterns, and pain. In difficult situations, forgiveness is the key to honorable closure, and I have experienced that forgiveness is possible even in the most brutal and tragic of circumstances.

I've witnessed a number of life-changing experiences where forgiveness transformed both the forgiver and the forgiven. Perhaps the most powerful example took place at the inauguration of Nelson Mandela as president of South Africa in May 1994. Having spent 27 years imprisoned by the apartheid regime, he had now assumed leadership of the nation nonviolently. The inauguration took place in a stadium where about 5,000 guests included leaders from all over the world. Hundreds of thousands of South Africans watched on jumbo screens outside the stadium. Mandela's speech was memorable and was widely quoted, but I felt that what happened after the inaugural ceremony was even more remarkable.

After the ceremony, we guests were invited to a gigantic green lawn adjacent to the stadium, full of round tables with white tablecloths, where we were served brunch by high school students in their school uniforms. Mandela sat at the head table between Prince Philip of Great Britain and Prime Minister Benazir Bhutto of Pakistan. At a certain point, Mandela clanked his glass, stood up, and asked the prince and the prime minister to move their chairs over a bit, and waiters brought over two more chairs next to him. Then he called over two men, large, somewhat portly

Afrikaners. I have not seen or read a written report of what happened then, but this is how I remember what he said:

> *I want everybody to meet my jailers. I was in prison for 27 years. My three activities were solitary confinement, hard labor, investigation and torture. I had three jailers. Two of them are alive and here with me today. They really are the only people I saw for most of those 27 years, and for the first 17 years, I hated them. Every brief encounter that we had was filled with hatred. In the 17th year of my imprisonment, I realized that such hate was unhealthy for me and for the movement. I realized if I spent the rest of my life in prison that I would die from hatred if I didn't find a way through. Most importantly, I realized that to free my people, I needed to free not only the oppressed but the oppressor. The oppressor is in a different kind of pain, a different kind of trauma, but just as horrendous as the oppressed. I needed to unlock the hatred by finding a place in my heart for my jailers. So I spent the next year, the 17th year of my imprisonment, learning to love these men. By the end of that year, I knew about their families, their wives, their parents. I found a place in my heart for them and I loved them. That's when I began to run the movement from prison.*

Then he introduced them by name, stood in front of them, and said, "Please forgive me for my years of hatred of you." I could see the tears streaming down their faces as they also asked him for his forgiveness for everything they did to him. He turned to the crowd, and as the three of them stood together, he said, "On this forgiveness we will build a new nation."

There followed in South Africa a new and very different context for moving forward after war, oppression, and the hatred and bigotry of apartheid. It was the beginning of the spirit of the truth and reconciliation process that later was established to bring Black and white South Africans together. The opening that came from Mandela's forgiveness—of his jailers as well as his former enemy F. W. de Klerk—brought forth a formal Truth and Reconciliation Commission not only in South Africa but also in a number of other countries.

FORGIVING THE UNFORGIVABLE

Many years later, in connection with my work with the Nobel Women's Initiative, I spent several days witnessing the proceedings of a truth and reconciliation process in the West African nation of Liberia. Decades of civil war had torn the country apart, killing, displacing, and traumatizing hundreds of thousands of people. Christian and Muslim women, led by Leymah Gbowee, came together to create a coalition that nonviolently pressured the government to pursue peace talks. In a remarkable movement, the women brought an end to two decades of war. (This amazing story is told in the film *Pray the Devil Back to Hell*, one of the most inspiring documentaries I have ever seen.)

During the days I watched the truth and reconciliation proceedings, I heard the horrific story of a family whose young daughter had been raped and killed in front of them and who were then beaten themselves by two soldiers. What happened when victims and perpetrators came together in the session I witnessed was astonishing. The soldiers had been children themselves at the time, drugged and dehumanized by the war. In tears, they took complete responsibility for what they had done, asked for forgiveness, and pledged to restore the daughter's honor and memory. Somehow, the parents were able to forgive them. They embraced the two men and they all cried together—as did all of us who were present. Later I came to understand that they had become like a family, turning their guilt and shame and hatred into love—clearing the past to make way for the future. Witnessing this event, my heart was broken open and I realized that with forgiveness anything is possible.

I have also had the privilege of knowing remarkable individuals whose capacity for forgiveness is stunning and inspiring. One is the amazing Azim Khamisa. In 1995, his only son, a 20-year-old student named Tariq, was shot and killed while delivering a pizza to an apartment of gang members in South Central Los Angeles. The killer, Tony Hicks, was only 14 years old and had been told by the gang that he had to prove himself by carrying out the killing. Despite his age, Tony was the first 14-year-old to be tried as an adult in the state of California and was sentenced to 25 years in prison.

Azim was devastated, of course, but as a Sufi Muslim, he sought solace in his faith, which guided him to forgiveness. Azim says he realized that his son's killer was just a child himself, that "there was a victim at both ends of that gun."

Azim reached out to Tony's grandfather and guardian, Ples Felix, who was also grieving and who welcomed their connection. Together they created the Tariq Khamisa Foundation to foster forgiveness and break the cycle of youth violence. Azim came to know of Tony's childhood of abuse and abandonment, and five years on, he visited Tony in prison and befriended him as well. They stayed in touch while he was in prison, and Azim advocated for his release. When Tony was released in 2019,

Azim offered him a job with the foundation, and he joined with his grandfather Ples and Azim in working to save the lives of other young souls. Tony has also become close to Tariq's sister, Tasreen, who welcomed him into the family after uncovering what she calls "layers to forgiveness."

THE COURAGE TO
ASK FOR FORGIVENESS

I can only imagine the depths of love that must be plumbed to find forgiveness for the killer of your son or brother. I also acknowledge the courage it takes to ask for forgiveness. I have seen this displayed by my dear friend and Pachamama Alliance cofounder John Perkins. Prior to his life as a champion for Indigenous people in the Amazon, John had a career as what is called an "economic hit man." His best-selling 2004 book, *Confessions of an Economic Hit Man*, tells the shocking inside story of how America took over the world.

For years in the 1960s and 1970s, John was chief economist at a US consulting firm working for institutions like the World Bank and USAID to persuade leaders of developing countries to accept enormous development loans for huge infrastructure projects like dams and highways. Then, saddled with massive debt, those countries could be forced to comply with pressures from the United States on any number of issues. Big US corporations that built the projects profited, while the debt load crippled the countries' economies and widened their wealth gap. As he saw the impact of his work, John struggled with his conscience and quit that world in 1981. He transformed his life, helped found the Pachamama Alliance, and became a global advocate for what he calls "a life economy as opposed to a death economy."

John's book had revealed the role he played in saddling Ecuador with debt, and many years later, he returned to the country to make a public apology for the terrible damage that he and the system he had worked for helped cause there. The apology occurred at a public gathering of a couple of thousand people in Quito in 2007 and was documented in a film called *Apology of an Economic Hit Man*, which was produced by a Greek filmmaker and was very popular in Europe. As John came onto the stage, there were cries of "Kill John Perkins!" but as he spoke, the crowd calmed down. He accepted full responsibility for "selling colonialism and exploitation," and soon the audience was cheering him.

For John, the public apology was a relief and a catharsis. Even though the Ecuadorean government bears responsibility for its decisions, he was able to speak the truth to the people he loved and to release decades of guilt. That gathering could have turned out much differently, but John's courage and integrity not only set him free but went a long way toward helping people in Ecuador and other countries understand something many Americans fail to see: the harm that US corporations sometimes cause in the world.

CLOSURE THROUGH
CEREMONY AND RITUAL

The clarity that comes from asking for forgiveness, receiving forgiveness, and going through the process of honorable closure creates the space for new openings and opportunities. Trying to operate on top of unfinished business and unacknowledged harmful actions can undercut good intentions and derail positive projects. Clearing and closure pave the way for our best efforts to succeed.

One path to closure is ceremony and ritual. Rituals of all kinds are beautiful markers that release one chapter and initiate another in our lives. I have witnessed this process many times over many years, especially in our Pachamama Alliance Journeys program. Since the mid-1990s, we have taken small groups (10 to 20 people) on two-week trips to Ecuador into the Amazon rainforest and into the Andes mountains. In both places, they have the opportunity to interact with the Indigenous people and to participate in profound ceremonies with shamans. It's a powerful and intense experience that binds participants in a tribe of sorts and invariably creates a transformation in their lives. At the end of each trip, we create a ritual that embodies the process of completion creating new openings.

Having slept and eaten meals in an Indigenous village, walked through the forest with local guides, swam in rivers with pink dolphins, communed with exotic birds and wildlife, and shared in life-changing medicine journeys with a shaman, our journeyers often complete the trip with a sacred ritual at a mountain ecolodge. We provide a small cloth made locally and bowls of beautiful things that represent parts of the journey: pebbles from the Andes that represent the magic and power of the mountains, rich soil from the rainforest, white flowers for purity, rose petals for love, local coins for prosperity, rosemary for remembrance, and cloves for the spice of life. The participants collect these talismans in their cloth and tie it with twine to create what we call their "commitment bundle."

In a semicircle around a fireplace, each person stands before the souls they have shared this time with, bundle in hand. First, they articulate their personal transformational experience to those who witnessed it. Then they acknowledge and give gratitude for the space and grace that fostered that transformation.

And third, they speak their commitment—stating specifically the actions they will take to anchor their transformation in action in the world. Inspired by the mission of the Pachamama Alliance, they speak about how they will contribute to an environmentally sustainable, spiritually fulfilling, and socially just future for all life. Often these actions are completely life changing—a new career or job, a step into politics or philanthropy, major lifestyle changes, new sustainable business projects and practices. In the months and sometimes years to come, the tribe stays connected and reports to each other about their progress, having made their pledge in this holy and communal ceremony.

When you commit to making a difference with your life, you enter the realm of the sacred. You honor your passages, your ups and downs, as experiences to serve the highest good. Honorable closure and forgiveness encourage growth and learning and foster freedom, fulfillment, and the deepening of your heart.

PART IV

Creating Your Committed Life

*To create your own committed life you need an ecosystem
of support including mindsets and skills, as well as an
understanding of your role as an evolutionary activist.*

CHAPTER 14

Support for Your Stand

*Don't ask yourself what the world needs. Ask yourself what
makes you come alive, and go do that, because what the
world needs is people who have come alive.*

—HOWARD THURMAN

In this last section, I offer some wisdom and support to you in
discovering and taking the stand that is appropriate to who
you are and also getting the support you need to follow through
on your commitment. I recognize that you may already be living
a commitment, deeply engaged in a purpose larger than yourself, and what you need is validation and encouragement. Or
you may be searching for that purpose or for greater commitment, seeking to expand it or to be more effective. Perhaps you
are just waking up to the state of the world and wanting to do
something that makes a difference for our future. This chapter
will help you create the architecture that can support your committed life.

DISCOVERING YOUR STAND

In thinking about what you are committed to in life, what is the larger stand that you are drawn to? I love Howard Thurman's quote about what makes you come alive, as it expresses the heart of the matter. When you "come alive," you experience your passion and are in your power. As a child or young person, what qualities were natural to you? If you were on the playground witnessing someone being bullied and you raced over to help the person, it might be a sign that you are a person who stands for justice. You might be a stand for all people to have respect and have a voice. If in your teen years you loved being in Nature, hiking, skiing, surfing, you may be a stand for the preservation of wilderness or the ocean. If you've been someone who loves singing, playing an instrument, or painting, you might be a stand for making sure that all children have access to music and the arts in school and in their lives.

If you look to see who your heroes and heroines have been, you'll get clues to your stand. As a little girl, my daughter Summer loved animals and couldn't bear to see them mistreated. Her heroine was Jane Goodall. She loved her and read everything about her. She wanted to be a veterinarian. She realized that she was a stand for all of life—not just human life—to be loved and cared for. Who are the people you most admire now, who most touch your heart? Look at the through line of your life: what has called to you? It doesn't matter if you call it a stand, a commitment, or a purpose, or whether you come up with one thing or five—the point is that if you ask, you will receive.

I believe that every person is born to express their talent and treasure in the direction of forging a better world. There is no one not in that category. Many people are blocked from it, blind to it, or numb to it, or have been hijacked by trauma, greed, envy, negativity, or even evil. But I assert that most people crave to stand for something that benefits all humanity and the future of life. And it is one of my stands to be with people in a way that they are in touch with that longing and discover what they stand for and begin to express it.

DREAMING BIG

No matter whether you are a seasoned activist or newly inspired to find your passion, I urge you, above all, to dream big. Don't be afraid to envision a commitment that feels scary, maybe even impossible. It was Walt Disney who said, "If you can dream it, you can do it."

A great deal of what I know about success I have learned from Jack Canfield, who has taught success principles to hundreds of thousands of people throughout the world. From an early age, Jack's dream was to reach millions of people with strategies to improve their lives. He achieved fame and fortune with the series of books called *Chicken Soup for the Soul*, collections of inspirational stories on a range of topics.

Jack's goal for the first book in the series was that it would become a best seller and reach millions of readers. Even though the book was rejected by 144 publishers, he did not give up. When it was finally in print, it was so successful that it launched a publishing empire: the series has been translated into 47 languages and has sold over half a billion books worldwide. Most important, hundreds of millions of lives have been touched and transformed by those books.

Dreaming, of course, is only the beginning. At this time in history, when we are being called upon to tackle gigantic problems, big dreams may need huge, transformational organizational efforts to execute them. My friend and colleague Dan Pallotta has inspired me to think newly about what is needed to solve what he calls our "labyrinth of social problems." He offers the example of the Apollo mission that put a man on the moon within nine years of President John F. Kennedy's commitment in 1961. It was an audacious goal with an impossible deadline, and it was accomplished by the unprecedented organization, coordination, and collaboration that was NASA. He calls on nonprofits in particular to abandon humble, incremental thinking and fear of criticism and to embrace audacious possibilities. Whether you work in the nonprofit sector or the business world, his message about what it will take for successful action is crucial for our times.

CREATING AN ECOSYSTEM OF SUPPORT

A big commitment is rarely, perhaps never, accomplished alone or quickly. I've discovered that a committed life requires robust support systems over time. There have been times when I've questioned my commitment. Is it too big? Is it arrogant? Can I handle something this big? Can I really make this kind of a difference? At the same time, even in periods of overwhelm, I knew that my stand and commitment would carry me through. But in order to ensure that, I realized I needed support, an ecosystem of people and practices that could sustain and nourish me on my journey.

I initiated that ecosystem when I made my stand public to people around me. Speaking my stand created a new context for our relationship and enabled my family, friends, and colleagues to relate to me newly—to my stand rather than to my personality. My husband Bill has always believed in me and created an environment of trust and certainty. One of my close friends, Tracy Apple, who also worked for The Hunger Project in the early days, became my committed listener. Many others listened, advised, and held me to account for what I was standing for.

I've also relied on mentors and role models, who are people whose life and work you admire and whom you watch and listen to. My mother was always my role model, and for many years my primary mentor was Joan Holmes, who was the CEO of The Hunger Project. I have long admired Jane Goodall, who is 11 years older than I am, aiming to emulate how she navigates living a committed life in her 80s. I also aspire to follow in the footsteps of Joanna Macy, who at this writing is approaching 93 years old. An author, activist, and Buddhist scholar, she has been on the cutting edge of environmental issues for decades, bring ing a spiritual perspective through what she calls "The Work That Reconnects." I so admire her sense of possibility (what she calls "active hope"), her courageous leadership, her stamina, and her commitment to never giving up. I want to be like Jane and Joanna when I grow up!

COLLABORATION AND TEAMWORK

The strongest and most important part of my support ecosystem is teamwork. In the teams I've worked with, there was never a real hierarchy, but rather a group of people all committed and aligned to the same vision and goal yet playing different roles to attain it. If you're fortunate enough to be part of a team, invite them to give you honest feedback when they see you're off track. Leadership is an act of humility, listening, and surrender as much as it is being in charge. In an earlier chapter, I looked at what happens when people get stuck in a position that stops the action. I've found that to work successfully with others, I have to be able to get off my position again and again when necessary and when it moves the action forward.

I've learned a great deal about cooperation and collaboration working with our Indigenous partners in the Pachamama Alliance. We didn't really know what we were doing when we took that name, but now we understand that it was sort of a divine inspiration for how important it is to be an ally and build alliances. Based on their dreams and visions, the Achuar realized they would not prevail in their contact with Western industrialized society without having allies who could help them understand what they were getting into. So, the Pachamama Alliance is an alliance of Indigenous people from the Amazon rainforest and conscious, committed people from the Western world working together for the sustainability of life. I'm privileged to be involved with this initiative, which is the culmination of my work to leave a legacy of a healthy and flourishing world sourced in many ways by a healthy Amazon rainforest.

The way forward in the 21st century is collaboration—to labor together to bring all voices to the table to realize the collective guidance that can bring forth our hopes and fulfill our dreams.

CONNECTING TO SPIRIT

In my experience, burnout occurs not when I'm overworked or stressed, but rather when I am disconnected from Source, which to me means Spirit or the higher Self. Earlier, I introduced you to two of my great spiritual mentors who are shamans and leaders, Manari Ushigua of the Sápara people of Ecuador and Arkan Lushwala from the Quechua of Peru and also from the Native American Lakota tradition. From each I have learned that we can only solve the great problems we face by accessing the spiritual world as well as the material world.

Of course, we need to act on problems on the material plane, but if we neglect to connect with the spiritual dimension, we can actually end up reinforcing or exacerbating the problems. Of course, accessing the spiritual realm is not the only answer—it's not like you can pray away a tsunami or ask God to give you a million dollars. Yet engaging with spiritual power—our own deep soul or God or what I call "unseen allies"—can give us access to actions and solutions we might not otherwise be aware of or relate to. Often that unseen ally is our own self—an inner knowing that shows itself when called upon.

I recall coaching a woman who was in great financial distress, having accumulated about $150,000 in credit card debt. She was experiencing such shame and fear that she was practically immobilized. I realized that she had become her debt—she and her debt were inseparable. I told her that before we could even begin to work on her debt issue, she needed to do an assignment. I asked her to acknowledge out loud and appreciate every person who crossed her path every day for the next week. At first, she was mystified and reluctant. She asked, "What does this have to do with my debt?" I said, "Trust me, just do it, and we'll talk next week."

At our next session, she told me she had had one of the most inspiring and powerful weeks of her life. She took her attention off herself and started to see the beauty in other people. She reconnected with her love for humanity and the opportunity to be of service to other people. She felt like she was a whole and complete person who had debt, rather than the debt having her. She had connected with who she was—her own spirit—and retrieved her personal power. From there she had the agency to go to work on her debt problem. Within two years, she not only was debt free but had saved $100,000.

LISTENING TO
INDIGENOUS WISDOM

Another great lesson from my Indigenous partners is the necessity of community—community with other people and as well as with all of life. While the Western industrialized world emphasizes hyper-individualism in a *you or me* world, the Indigenous way of life is built around sufficiency, sharing, reciprocity, and community. They live in a *you and me* world. The highest ethic for them is what is good for the community, and within that way of life, all individuals are cared for. In the Western world, we individuate at the expense of each other and at the expense of the community of life and the natural world itself.

In keeping with their more spiritual perspective, my mentors have inspired me to question how we in the modern world relate to time. Many of us are completely at the mercy of our schedules and our devices. My Indigenous colleagues refuse to rush. They have an unbelievable reverence for time. Hurrying would not occur to them, except in an emergency, and then they can run as fast as the wind. But they refuse to rush falsely, whereas I seem to be constantly in a hurry to get on to the next thing. When I am with Arkan or Manari, they are fully present with me, with nothing going on. They are not thinking about what just happened or what is next. Their capacity to be here now is really stunning to me.

Often the Indigenous way of knowing is called ancient wisdom or Earth-based wisdom: knowledge that has been sourced from the natural world and been passed down orally through each generation. It recognizes the miraculous workings of Nature and attributes to animals, plants, forests, mountains, and bodies of water what we humans call *souls*. The wisdom of the Earth is that everything is sacred. What a beautiful way to live!

CEREMONY AND RITUAL

In a world that is almost completely digitized, I've seen that the more digital we become, the more ritual we need. Another great teaching I have absorbed from my Indigenous friends is the importance of ceremony and ritual, not only in our personal lives but also in our organizations and companies. Ceremonies and rituals bring significance and meaning to events and passages. Many of us are familiar with personal rituals like meditating, praying, doing yoga, lighting candles for a loved one, or anything we do regularly in a prescribed way that brings us into contact with the sacred.

When I'm about to begin a coaching session, I bring out my little Yoda figurine and rub his head as a source for connecting with and imparting my wisdom. When I'm fundraising and about to ask for a significant amount of money, I light a candle and meditate on the person involved. Sometimes I walk in the redwood grove near our house and derive inspiration from the magnificence of these ancient trees. When I stand facing one of these great beings and ask for guidance, I invariably receive it. Being near or in the ocean is also a source of great sustenance for me.

I now look for ways to bring ritual and ceremony into my family life as well as into my workplaces. When groups gather for meetings or events at the Pachamama Alliance and the Soul of Money Institute, we begin with what we call "opening sacred space." Someone generally leads a short meditation that enables us to become physically and mentally present, to honor the land on which we are located as well as its original residents, and to ask for guidance from seen and unseen allies to help us accomplish the purpose of our time together.

We also add to our opening ritual a personal check-in process, where each person has a few moments to speak and be seen, to express anything that might be in the way of being present or share something that might give juice to the group process. On many occasions we end the meeting with appreciations, noticing, and speaking about what mattered to us, what happened, or what someone said that was valuable or uplifting. Instead of just thinking about the next thing to do, people head back to their desks or tasks feeling good, feeling inspired, and feeling seen.

PRACTICING GRATITUDE

The twin to appreciation is gratitude, celebrating what's been given to you rather than what you've produced. To be grateful requires some humility, some acceptance of grace. The practice of gratitude has been the most potent and meaningful ritual of my life. For many years I have kept a gratitude journal, ending the day by writing down five things I am grateful for. It never fails to lift me out of my petty concerns and remind me how blessed I am. During the COVID-19 pandemic times, my entire 11-member family—Bill and I, our kids, and our grandkids— participated in a nightly ritual of posting in an email five things each of us felt grateful for that day. This was when I discovered who my family really were, what they cared about, what caught their attention each day, and what really mattered to them.

OWNING PROGRESS
AND SAVORING SUCCESS

Sometimes we are so caught up in what still needs to be done to accomplish our commitment that we neglect this very important aspect of self-support: owning progress. Keeping score is a really important part of the game! And while we are often completely ready to ding ourselves when we haven't scored, we may forget to chalk up our points when we have a win. Sometimes we treat a great event as an aberration or just some good luck rather than progress. I think of the military metaphor of taking territory or the football image of moving the ball down the field. Every bit of ground gained counts.

How often, at the end of a day's work, do we congratulate ourselves on what we *did* do rather than berate ourselves for what we didn't get done? At the end of a meeting, coaching session, or gathering, rather than just looking at what needs to be done next, I ask participants to reflect on and state what has been accomplished.

Even as a society, we rarely allow ourselves to notice, much less celebrate, the progress that is being made in almost every realm of life. For many years, at the end of every year, *New York Times* columnist Nicholas Kristof has written "Why [This Year] Was the Best Year in Human History." As an antidote to the gloom and doom of most of the news, he offers evidence that each year the world's population is living longer and living better than ever before. He gives specific data regarding decreases in poverty, hunger, and child mortality and increases in life expectancy, literacy, and access to technology. In 2019, he wrote, "So there's plenty to fret about. But a failure to acknowledge global progress can leave people feeling hopeless and ready to give up. In fact, the gains should show us what is possible and spur greater efforts to improve opportunity worldwide."

Our reluctance to claim progress may seem like it will motivate us—like we can't let ourselves off the hook; we have to keep plugging away. But if we don't take the opportunity to stop, breathe, smile, and congratulate ourselves on even part of a job well done, burnout will take its toll. Savoring success strengthens who you are and allows you to own your accomplishments, not out of pride or arrogance but with the humility of feeling privileged to do the work you have taken on. It may take speaking it to another person, writing it down in a journal, or throwing a party, but acknowledging the progress that has occurred as a result of your effort, participation, and leadership is central to the warp and weave of a committed life.

BEING A CLEARING

If your commitment is rooted in your stand for your life and you can feel it in your body, you'll have the strength and capacity to stay the course no matter what is happening or how long it takes. There are many visions I've had and projects I've worked on that have taken years to manifest.

I think of how when we first began working with the Achuar people in the Ecuadorean Amazon, I felt so strongly that the Achuar women were marginalized and oppressed by the warrior culture. They were expected to bear many children, take care of everything for the family, and constantly serve the needs of the men. They had no outlets for self-expression, seemed constantly exhausted, and had very little say in community life. As mentioned previously, their birthing practices unnecessarily endangered mothers and babies. I so wanted them to be able

to live differently—to know their value and power and have a
voice. I recognized my arrogance, however, and since they did
not request any guidance or help, I had to let go of my agenda
for them. Still, I knew that every human being longs to be seen
and valued, so over the years I held that vision for the women
in my heart.

It took 10 years for an opening to occur: the request by Achuar women for help with safer birthing practices, which became
a highly successful community health project run by the women
themselves. Over the past 15 years, their involvement with
Ikiama Nukuri has transformed the role of women in Achuar
society. They now hold leadership positions in their organizations and participate fully in community life.

I am well aware that I will probably not live to see the accomplishment of other major commitments of my life. When I
started with The Hunger Project, we declared the goal of ending
hunger by the end of the century—the 20th century. It hasn't
ended, but it is on that trajectory. Currently, the Amazon rainforest is being destabilized as extractive industries have their way
with it, but the Amazon Sacred Headwaters Initiative is seeking
to turn things around. This Indigenous-led movement to put 85
million acres of rainforest in permanent protection is gaining
ground and may see miraculous results in the next decade. It
may indeed take another 75 years to manifest the Sophia Century, when the full power of the feminine is embraced and a
truly equal partnership of the sexes brings forth a more balanced
and thriving world.

What I have begun to appreciate, however, is that no matter
how long it takes, I am a space or a clearing in which something
can happen. Being a clearing combines the qualities of taking a stand and creating a context. You have a clear vision and

intention, although you may have no idea how you will accomplish it. Just holding that space creates the context in which the desired content can gestate and then come to life. Martin Luther King Jr. continues to be a clearing for bringing racial justice and equality to all. If something is true and wants to be born, it will show up in its time. I spoke earlier of the notion of creating "an idea whose time has come." Being a clearing has enormous power to facilitate an idea's time coming.

ASKING FOR HELP

Here is one last, simple piece of advice—the key to workability: When you run into trouble, are overwhelmed, or don't know what to do, ask for help! If we look at Nature, we can see that everything is connected—no species stands alone. Our misguided species often feels that we have to go it alone, but everything that works does so in an ecosystem of support. Rather than showing weakness, asking for help expresses your bigness. A committed life is only possible when you are big enough to ask for help.

CHAPTER 15

Cocreating an Evolutionary Leap

Another world is not only possible, she is on her way.
On a quiet day, I can hear her breathing.
—ARUNDHATI ROY

Perhaps you have heard the ancient Chinese curse "May you live in interesting times."

The times we live in are beyond interesting; they are tumultuous and frightening. The global mobilization needed to address the warming of the planet has barely achieved liftoff. We are on track to fulfill Buckminster Fuller's 1976 prediction that in about 50 years, all of the institutions of society would unravel and cease to serve us. It is evident that our political system—and even democracy itself—is falling apart at the seams. Our economic system benefits the very few at the expense of the very many. Our educational system doesn't serve its true constituents, our children. Our judicial system is held hostage to aggregated money and power. Even our religious institutions no longer seem relevant to a majority of people. The ground of being that humans have relied on for centuries is no longer stable. But is this a curse or a blessing?

My mentor, the Buddhist scholar, author, and activist Joanna Macy, says she feels blessed to be alive in these times. Now in her early 90s, she says she is grateful to witness the remarkable transition that she calls the Great Turning. She asserts that "souls are lining up hoping to incarnate" to be part of this evolutionary leap for the human family and for our species. Bucky Fuller also saw that system collapse, though painful, is necessary and appropriate: it creates an incredible opportunity to reimagine, reinvent, and rebuild our societal systems in order to create a world that works for everyone—and for all of life.

THE ROLE OF HUMANS NOW

Scientists now call our age the Anthropocene, the era when humans are determining the future of the planet. We human beings have become so powerful that we are no longer the objects of evolution, but rather humanity itself has become a powerful force in shaping life for everything on Earth, often creating disastrous unintended consequences. Now we need to become *evolutionary activists*—intentionally engaging with the momentum of evolution to shape the future we want. We need to collaborate with the forces that brought the universe into existence—to become instruments through which the evolutionary process works to create an epoch-level transformation.

In assuming the role of masters of the planet, we humans have lost our place in the universe. From this misleading mindset, we've given ourselves permission to extract, to dominate, and to destroy the very life support system we depend on and of which we are a part. We don't live *in* an ecosystem, we are part *of* an ecosystem. Yet, we do not even include ourselves as part of Nature. The Oxford Languages dictionary defines *nature* in this way: "[T]he phenomena of the physical world collectively, including plants, animals, the landscape, and other features and products of the earth, as opposed to humans or human creations."

If we are not part of Nature, what are we?

We humans are deeply rooted in something larger than ourselves. As the poet Rabindranath Tagore expressed it, "The same stream of life that runs through my veins night and day runs through the world."

HOSPICING AND MIDWIFING

Ending human supremacy, locating ourselves as part of Nature rather than above it, and embracing the sacredness of all of life means we are being called on to hospice the death of the old systems and midwife the birth of new ones. We can hospice the old with respect and gratitude for how well those structures served us at another time. We can midwife the new based on an entirely different relationship with our Mother Earth—what Thomas Berry calls "a mutually enhancing human-earth relationship." It is good to remember Buckminster Fuller's famous quote, "You never change things by fighting the existing reality. To change something, build a new model that makes the existing model obsolete."

What is needed now is not only new systems, but a new kind of human being, and it is my perspective that humanity is pregnant and about to give birth. If you came upon a woman giving birth, screaming in pain, and you did not know what was happening, you might think she was gravely injured or dying. Until the baby arrives, birthing is a harrowing process for the mother as well as witnesses. The birthing process is a great metaphor for our times and for our role as midwives of a new future.

Midwifing the future is an awesome challenge, but evolution is on our side. My Indigenous teachers say that even the COVID pandemic aims to serve us. It is not a punishment, they say, but rather an announcement, an ally meant to give our species the time and space to rethink, reimagine, and reset. Although I do not discount the awful reality of millions of deaths, I see the pandemic as a kind of morning sickness for a pregnant species.

It is the feminine that gives birth. In her book *Letters from the Infinite*, Rev. Deborah Johnson makes the distinction between building and birthing. When you build, you are picturing and creating an outcome that you can control, and you build what serves you. When you give birth, you are bringing into existence something that unfolds, something over which you have no control, and you seek to serve it. The capacity to build and control is the function of the masculine, and that ideal, that ethos, has dominated throughout most of human history. I believe we are at the beginning of the Sophia Century, when feminine knowledge and guidance—in both women and men—will hold and nourish the future. It is precisely the wisdom that is held in the feminine archetype that is needed to make the leap and give birth to a transformed world.

The tide is turning as women are showing up and leading in government, corporations, and other institutions. They are speaking up and challenging societal norms through many movements, such as #MeToo. Young women in particular have assumed the leadership of the climate action movement and Black Lives Matter. Yet, despite these achievements, the patriarchy continues to rule the world, and we have much work to do to bring masculine and feminine values into balance and fulfill the promise of the Sophia Century.

THE CATERPILLAR
AND THE BUTTERFLY

Who is this new kind of human now being born? It is actually a new way of seeing and being that is coming alive in all of us. A great metaphor for our times is the transformation of the caterpillar into a butterfly. When a caterpillar reaches a certain point in its evolution, it becomes overconsumptive, a voracious eater that consumes hundreds of times its own weight. At that same time, inside the molecular structure of the caterpillar, something called the imaginal cells become active. They wake up, look for each other, and begin to cluster inside the caterpillar's body. When enough of them connect, even though they are not in the majority, they become the genetic directors of the future of the caterpillar. At that point, the other cells begin to dissolve and become what's called the nutritive soup—out of which the imaginal cells create the absolutely unpredictable miracle of the butterfly.

I believe that those of us who are alive now—young, old, male, female—are the imaginal cells that are gathering together to create the next phase of human existence. It is from our imagination and vision that a miraculous transformation is occurring. We are all aware of the painful realities of our world in transition—the devastation that our overconsumption has caused. I've learned from two great ministers, Michael Beckwith and Deborah Johnson, that "pain pushes until vision pulls." Pain hurts and vision liberates. When vision begins to pull, pain begins to dissipate, and your attention and intention are given to the vision.

It is crucial that we have a vision that pulls us out of fear and despair and guides our actions. And it is also crucial that we dare to believe that that vision is possible. I'm inspired by big, bold visions that can't help but get you excited.

Paul Hawken has provided that kind of vision, first with his 2017 Project Drawdown, which demonstrated the possibility of "reversing global warming by 2050," and most recently with his 2021 book *Regeneration*, which is subtitled *Ending the Climate Crisis in One Generation*. Who but Paul is envisioning an actual end to the climate crisis?

PUTTING THE REGENERATION OF LIFE
AT THE CENTER OF EVERYTHING

Paul's concept of regeneration expands our understanding of how to respond to global warming by connecting it to our other human-made crises—social justice, inequality, and threats to democracy. Most important, it places love of life at the center of everything we do. The book and website (*regeneration.org*) provide guidance for what is needed now in dozens of human endeavors, including specific actions, projects, and organizations that enable anyone to integrate regeneration into their life.

Regeneration offers a context for finding your stand and living your committed life. It provides a vision that can pull us away from the pain of our past mistakes and the fear of the future. The greatest threat to creating the future we want is fear, discouragement, and cynicism. People are dis-couraged because they're disconnected from their own courage. They think somebody else is supposed to fix things, and those people aren't doing their job. They blame and become cynical. It's easy to be cynical. It's easy and cheap because it asks nothing of us. Cynicism is like a disease, an infection, and it's cowardly.

What takes courage is to hold a vision and live into it, to generate visionary conversations for other people that uplift them—that take them out of cynicism, negativity, and discouragement and connect them with their courage. Once you get back in touch with your own courage, you realize, "Oh, I can do something about this. I care. I have heart. I have power. I can act!" It is only in action that we can find hope; active hope becomes a beacon for our lives.

So, our vision must be clear and purposeful, powerful enough to pull us out of the trance that modern society has created, strong enough to overcome our pessimism and reluctance to change. The Great Awakening, the Great Turning, the Great Transition, and, indeed, a revolutionary Evolutionary Leap is underway. We humans were meant to survive and thrive on this planet—along with all the other magnificent life forms we share it with.

In our role as the ancestors of the future, our task could not be more compelling: our Great Work now is to ensure the future for all of life.

BREATHE AND PUSH

In closing, I return to our birth analogy. Author and activist Valarie Kaur, the creator of the Revolutionary Love Project, also correlates the birth process with our sometimes terrifying world. In her talks she asks, "Is this the darkness of the tomb or the darkness of the womb? . . . To give birth, the midwife tells us to breathe and then to push. Breathe and push. In all of our labors, the labor of raising a family, or making a movement, or birthing a new nation, we need people to help us breathe and push into the fires of our bodies and the fires in the world."

We are going to have to breathe and push our way through some very challenging times. We don't know how long this labor will be. It could be a 10-year birth or longer, but we would not be on this Earth now if we weren't the perfect people to navigate this passage. It is not a burden, not a have-to, but rather a privilege, an opportunity, to play full-out—to marshal all of our hearts, talents, and skills in service of birthing an ecological civilization. We were born for these times. And we get to give birth to a new world.

CONCLUSION

What Is Yours to Do?

Never doubt that a small group of thoughtful, committed citizens can change the world. Indeed, it is the only thing that ever has.

—MARGARET MEAD

So, where do you go from here? I recognize that there is a continuum of commitment, and that you may have lived your stand for many years, or you may be someone who is just beginning to search for a purpose larger than yourself.

If you are someone who has been in the trenches, I honor you and hope this book validates your life path and inspires you to keep giving your all. If you are on fire with your work and see it making a difference, more power to you! If you are struggling financially and you're feeling discouraged and exhausted, my heart goes out to you. You need a support structure and resources to get through tough times, but you also need to take care of yourself. There is a lovely quote from spiritual teacher Ma Jaya

Sati Bhagavati, "Learn to drink as you pour, so the spiritual heart cannot run dry and you always have love to give." "Drink as you pour" means give to yourself as you give to others. It's a form of arrogance to separate yourself from what you are trying to transform. Living in sacrifice just isn't sustainable, and it's inconsistent with a world that works for all. That world includes you!

Burnout is real, and I have been there many times. I used to think that taking care of myself was a form of selfishness, but I have since learned that self-care—ensuring your own health, well-being, and financial stability—is an act of responsibility and courage in the face of a commitment larger than your own life. In some circumstances, burnout is a sign of being disconnected from your Source. I've learned that the most powerful pathway to finding your energy and life force is connecting with whatever sourced you in the first place—what touched your heart and made you make the big commitments you've made. No matter how troubled, how upset, how literally spent you are, there's power in reconnecting with your vision and knowing that it still lives in your heart.

PURPOSE AND PATIENCE

If your life purpose and mission eludes you, be patient. I believe that everyone alive has a role to play in the great transformation that is occurring now. Open yourself to that possibility and live with the intention to have it show up. Let go of your doubts about yourself and focus on the difference you can make. There's a north star that's calling to you, and your openness, eagerness, and longing will create a clearing for it to show up when the time is right.

If you are just discovering your own passion and launching your own committed life, do you have to quit your job and upend your life in order to get into action? Perhaps. And perhaps launching a new life will be the most courageous and worthwhile thing you've ever done.

But I want to be clear that living your commitment does not mean you have to do something big and global. People who live their commitments are kindergarten teachers, nurses, firefighters, entrepreneurs, mothers—anyone who sees their life as a gift that they feel called to give in service. What is different is that your work and your life are now held in a larger context. You are focused not just on yourself and your job, but on the bigger picture—seeking to bring about systemic or transformational change. Committed people are the kindergarten teacher who takes on making sure that preschool is available to all in her community; the nurse who is organizing for better care policies; the firefighter who is researching and implementing new fire prevention modalities; the entrepreneur who is working on getting plastic out of the waste stream; the mother who inspires her children to know that they matter. It is not the size of the commitment, but the intention and focus: What is the fulfillment of your life's purpose—your "splendid torch" to hand on to future generations?

Whatever you seek to offer, find your "small group of thoughtful, committed citizens," and work together! Alone, we may struggle, but often, together we are a genius. Yes, there are single "influencers" who can make a difference, but the future of the planet will be determined by collective action: from local groups working at the grassroots to national organizations working to change policies to international movements for global transformation. At whatever level you choose to operate, getting connected to other changemakers is perhaps the most valuable action you can take. The great spiritual teacher Thich Nhat Hanh said, "The next Buddha will be a Sangha"—the word sangha meaning "group," "community," or "collective."

And so, if your committed life is not already underway, just get started. Keep in mind the lines from W. H. Murray:

> *Whatever you can do, or dream you can, begin it.*
> *Boldness has genius, power, and magic in it!*

WE ARE THE ONES
WE'VE BEEN WAITING FOR

When you commit to a vision larger than your own life, it may sound like an act of arrogance, but in actuality it is humbling. You are freed from the obsession with your own identity, comfort, and satisfaction, and you become the instrument of your commitment. It shapes you into the person you need to be. It creates a clearing for your life to have meaning. It demands that you collaborate with others, and you become a magnet for others of vision and commitment.

Being alive today means being in the presence of the greatest challenge humanity has ever faced: the long-term future of life. This is an all-hands-on-deck moment, a calling to transform the way we live and regenerate our human systems so that all life on Earth can not only survive but flourish.

A committed life may not be everyone's path, but I know we need more people living this way. Given the enormous challenges facing humanity now, it will take millions of us willing to dream big, take risks, and face uncertainty with courage. If you have made it to the end of this book, it's clear that you are one of those people. This is the moment, and as the Hopi prophecy says, "We are the ones we have been waiting for."

Living a Committed Life
DISCUSSION AND
REFLECTION GUIDE

These questions can guide a group discussion or inspire deeper introspection by individual readers.

Introduction

Lynne Twist says that living a committed life is crucial to our human future. How do you relate to having a "purpose larger than yourself"?

How do you feel about the future, and what do you think is most needed in these times?

PART I: THE POWER OF COMMITMENT

Chapter 1: A Splendid Torch

How does the George Bernard Shaw quote affect you? What do you feel after reading it?

What does the word *commitment* mean to you?

What are you most committed to in life and why?

Chapter 2: Guidance from Source

Lynne Twist speaks as someone whose guidance comes from Spirit or Source. Where do you find guidance in your life?

Think about or share an experience of how guidance has shaped your life.

If you are not a spiritual person, how do you relate to the notion of faith in higher or divine forces? Where does your faith lie?

Chapter 3: Answering the Call

Have you heard a call or calls to engage with something larger than yourself?

What are the values that generate your desire to serve?

As you contemplate your own purpose and commitment, what life experiences have you had that guide and empower you?

Chapter 4: Taking a Stand

Have you taken a stand for what calls to you?

How does the distinction between stand and position resonate with you?

Have you experienced having to get off of a position in order to forward the action?

How do you express what you stand for in your day-to-day life?

PART II: THE SOUL OF COMMITMENT

Chapter 5: Transformation

How does the difference between change and transformation occur to you?

Lynne Twist says that in a transformative experience, things show up differently and actions flow from a new context. Think about or share an experience of transformation in your life.

Who do you consider to be the transformational figures or leaders of our time?

What area(s) of life would you most like to see transformed?

Chapter 6: Context: The Power of Story

Lynne Twist says that a shift in context—essentially telling a new story—reshapes content and redefines reality. If you have had such an experience in your life, contemplate it or share about it.

Have you experienced shifting from something happening *to* you to something happening *for* you? What difference did it make?

Chapter 7: The Magic of Possibility

Would you call yourself a possibilist? If not, what is in the way of embracing grounded optimism?

Who or what opens up possibility and gives you hope for the future?

Chapter 8: Breakdown into Breakthrough

Think about or share about a breakdown that became a breakthrough that you have experienced or witnessed. How did it impact your life?

What are you taking away from this chapter that may help you transform a difficult situation?

Chapter 9: From Scarcity to Sufficiency

To what degree have the myths of scarcity and "more is better" impacted your life?

What is in the way of experiencing your own sufficiency?

How do you relate to the practice of gratitude? What value might it have for you?

PART III: CHALLENGES, CHANGE, AND COMPLETION

Chapter 10: Being Tested

What challenges do you face in living a committed life?

What has been most useful for you in dealing with over-commitment and overwhelm?

Has illness ever had a positive impact on your life?

Chapter 11: Being Proximate to Suffering

Think about or share about an instance in which you were proximate to suffering. How did it impact you?

Often we try to avoid witnessing suffering. What is the value of engaging with it?

When have you had a moment of sorrow or hurt that has been healed by being witnessed by another?

Chapter 12: Loss, Failure, and Resilience

How does this chapter help you see failure in a new light?

Think about or share about a time of loss or failure in your life: Did it strengthen or debilitate you?

Chapter 13: Closure, Forgiveness, and New Openings

What impacted you most about the process of honorable closure?

When and how have you been empowered by forgiveness—giving it or receiving it?

How might ceremony or ritual contribute to your work and life?

PART IV: CREATING YOUR COMMITTED LIFE

Chapter 14: Support for Your Stand

What are the strengths and weaknesses of your current "ecosystem of support"?

What advice did you find most useful in this chapter?

Chapter 15: Cocreating an Evolutionary Leap

What does it mean to you to become an *evolutionary activist*?

What does *regeneration* mean to you, and where might you focus on "putting life at the center of all our actions"?

Conclusion: What Is Yours to Do?

Where are you on the path of creating your committed life?

What impact has this book had on getting you into action?

RESOURCES

The Pachamama Alliance
If you are seeking to join with other like-minded souls and to be in action, I recommend the Pachamama Alliance. We are a global community offering transformational educational programs and training in community-based climate action as well as a profound connection to preserving the Amazon rainforest. That work includes teachings from Indigenous shamans and leaders and life-changing journeys to the Ecuadorean Amazon. Becoming a "Pacha-person" will enhance your life and your impact. Learn more at *pachamama.org*.

The Soul of Money Institute
The Soul of Money Institute addresses the dysfunction and suffering that most people have in their relationship with money in order to bring a new level of consciousness to the way money impacts our life and society. My partner Sara Vetter and our team offer transformational workshops and courses, as well as coaching and consulting to organizations and individuals. We

also provide fundraising trainings and programs for the empowerment of women. Contact us at *soulofmoney.org*.

The Nobel Women's Initiative

I have the honor of serving as a fundraiser and consultant for
this remarkable organization of women who have received
the Nobel Peace Prize: Rigoberta Menchú Tum, Jody Williams, Shirin Ebadi, Tawakkol Karman, and Leymah Gbowee.
Through this initiative, these courageous women bring their
extraordinary experiences and work to spotlighting, amplifying,
and promoting the work of grassroots women's organizations
and movements around the world, and to strengthening and
expanding feminist efforts to promote nonviolent solutions to
war, violence, and militarism. You can learn about and support
us at *nobelwomensinitiative.org*.

The Hunger Project

Since 1977, The Hunger Project has been a pioneering global
organization committed to ending hunger and poverty worldwide through sustainable, grassroots, and women-centered strategies. Hunger Project programs in Africa, South Asia, and Latin
America are holistic, innovative, and highly effective, with three
core principles: start with women, mobilize communities, and
engage government. You can get involved and donate at *thp.org*.

Amazon Sacred Headwaters Initiative

The Amazon Sacred Headwaters Initiative aims to put one of the
most biodiverse regions of the planet into permanent protection.
It is a remarkable collaboration of Indigenous people, the philan-
thropic community, NGOs, social entrepreneurs, governments,

and the private sector to establish a region of Ecuador and Peru as off-limits to large-scale resource extraction. The vision is that this 85-million-acre area will be governed in accordance with traditional Indigenous principles of cooperation, harmony, and reverence for all life. Learn more at *sacredheadwaters.org*.

ACKNOWLEDGMENTS

I am deeply grateful to so many people for this book but moreover for the life I've been privileged to lead. The person who has given me the most space, encouragement, and permission to be who I am is my husband, my anchor, my confidant, and the love of my life, Bill Twist. He has stood by me and for me in every way for more than 50 years.

I also thank my adult children, Basil, Summer, and Zachary Twist, for believing in me. I am grateful for my five amazing grandchildren, Ayodele Abdul Hadi, Isa Twist, Ibrahim Twist, Jacqueline Joy Foley, and Ivy Rose Foley, for constantly inspiring me and standing with me for the future of their dreams.

This book would not have been written without the awesome partnership of my longtime friend and collaborative writer Mary Earle Chase. Her insight, skill, dedication, and, most of all, love for me and the message I carry has been a gift beyond measure.

My dear friend and one of my greatest mentors, Jack Canfield, originally suggested I write this book and sat me down in his living room to begin telling the stories that are the architecture and bones of this message. His encouragement of my work has been steadfast and generous, as has the support of my friends in the Transformational Leadership Council, which Jack founded.

Steve Piersanti, my editor, and the entire team at Berrett-Koehler Publishers have been nothing short of fantastic. It was my good friend John Perkins, a best-selling author and cofounder of the Pachamama Alliance, who encouraged me to publish with Berrett-Koehler. He knew it was the right choice for me. Thank you, John!

Van Jones, Ocean and John Robbins, Paul Hawken, Rev. Deborah Johnson, Hafsat Abiola, Joanna Macy, and Linda Curtis made significant contributions to the book, as did my partner in the Soul of Money Institute, Sara Vetter. Sara makes everything I do possible and keeps me smiling, laughing, and having fun along the way. The multitalented Mikey Gunderson keeps us both on track. Zachary Twist, Carolyn Buck Luce, Tammy White, and Tracy Maes as well have been invaluable partners in the Soul of Money Institute.

I am deeply grateful to the Nobel Peace Prize laureates I have worked with in the Nobel Women's Initiative. Their courage and resilience in the face of nearly insurmountable odds are inspiring beyond words.

All of my friends and colleagues at the Pachamama Alliance gave me space not only to write the book, but to do the work that made this message possible. I so appreciate our talented staff, generous donors, and phenomenal board of directors, chaired by Catherine Parrish.

My dear friend Tracy Apple has always been at my side, encouraging me and holding me to account in all that I do with her great wisdom and integrity.

Our work in the Sacred Headwaters of the Amazon rainforest, brilliantly led by Belen Paez and Atossa Soltani, and supported by the amazing Daniel Koupermann, has connected me to inspiring Indigenous people there who have shown me a whole new way of looking at the world. Manari Ushigua, Domingo Peas, and Narcisa Mashienta have been powerful partners in Ecuador. My teacher Arkan Lushwala has enriched and guided my life as well as the Pachamama Alliance organization.

I have profound appreciation for all of the people I have worked with: my coaches, coaching clients past and present, the participants in my courses, and particularly the women who have been part of the Remarkable Women's Journey. Their love and commitment to making a difference with their lives is deeply inspiring.

One more nod to the late Buckminster Fuller and to Werner Erhard, Joan Holmes, and Jim Garrison, who cut down the tall grass in front of me so that I could walk this powerful path. Thank you.

INDEX

ABOUT THE AUTHOR

by Mary Earle Chase

To encounter Lynne Twist is to have your life changed, your perspective shifted, your pessimism shaken, your heart opened. In fact, there are two kinds of people in the world: those who have fallen in love with Lynne and those who have never met her. Hundreds of thousands of people have heard her speak, taken her courses, watched her interviewed by Oprah, and read her book. She is known as one of the most inspiring transformational leaders of our time.

I met Lynne more than four decades ago and have had the great privilege of working closely with her throughout many of those years, including collaborating with her on this book. I know these "about the author" pieces usually focus on achievements and awards, but I aim to convey to you a fuller picture of this remarkable woman.

If you have read this book, you will know of her accomplishments, that she has committed her life to service: she has raised hundreds of millions of dollars to end hunger on the planet; she galvanized world leaders to cooperate at the end of the Cold War; she founded a global organization dedicated to saving the rainforest as well as changing the destructive dream of the modern world; she helped organize and fund women Nobel Peace Prize laureates; she is the author of *The Soul of Money*, a book that transformed readers' relationship with money and with themselves; her Soul of Money Institute has elevated fundraising to a new level of meaning and effectiveness and empowered women to step up to leadership roles in what she calls the Sophia Century. Not reported in this book are the stories of hundreds of people she has shepherded through life-changing journeys to the Amazon rainforest and coaching clients whose lives she has uplifted and transformed. Some would call her their spiritual teacher.

And during this time, Lynne has raised three accomplished children, contributed greatly to five grandchildren, celebrated 50-plus years of an enviable marriage, and interacted with many of the world's most powerful and prominent people.

These accomplishments don't quite convey, however, the unique gift this woman is to the world. Yes, Lynne is unstoppable in achieving her commitments, but she does so with humility, open-hearted grace, and indefatigable enthusiasm. She is boundlessly generous—with her time, her inspiration, and even her own home. She does not distinguish between those deserving of her love and attention and those who are not: all are welcome and appreciated for who they are in Lynne Twist land. She loves to laugh, dance, and celebrate the good in the world.

May she find her way into your heart as she has into mine.

MARY EARLE CHASE *is a writer and media producer whose work is focused on empowering people to heal the planet.*

Berrett–Koehler
Publishers

Berrett-Koehler is an independent publisher dedicated to an ambitious mission: *Connecting people and ideas to create a world that works for all.*

Our publications span many formats, including print, digital, audio, and video. We also offer online resources, training, and gatherings. And we will continue expanding our products and services to advance our mission.

We believe that the solutions to the world's problems will come from all of us, working at all levels: in our society, in our organizations, and in our own lives. Our publications and resources offer pathways to creating a more just, equitable, and sustainable society. They help people make their organizations more humane, democratic, diverse, and effective (and we don't think there's any contradiction there). And they guide people in creating positive change in their own lives and aligning their personal practices with their aspirations for a better world.

And we strive to practice what we preach through what we call "The BK Way." At the core of this approach is *stewardship,* a deep sense of responsibility to administer the company for the benefit of all of our stakeholder groups, including authors, customers, employees, investors, service providers, sales partners, and the communities and environment around us. Everything we do is built around stewardship and our other core values of *quality, partnership, inclusion,* and *sustainability.*

This is why Berrett-Koehler is the first book publishing company to be both a B Corporation (a rigorous certification) and a benefit corporation (a for-profit legal status), which together require us to adhere to the highest standards for corporate, social, and environmental performance. And it is why we have instituted many pioneering practices (which you can learn about at www.bkconnection.com), including the Berrett-Koehler Constitution, the Bill of Rights and Responsibilities for BK Authors, and our unique Author Days.

We are grateful to our readers, authors, and other friends who are supporting our mission. We ask you to share with us examples of how BK publications and resources are making a difference in your lives, organizations, and communities at www.bkconnection.com/impact.

Dear reader,

Thank you for picking up this book and welcome to the worldwide BK community! You're joining a special group of people who have come together to create positive change in their lives, organizations, and communities.

What's BK all about?

Our mission is to connect people and ideas to create a world that works for all.

Why? Our communities, organizations, and lives get bogged down by old paradigms of self-interest, exclusion, hierarchy, and privilege. But we believe that can change. That's why we seek the leading experts on these challenges—and share their actionable ideas with you.

A welcome gift

To help you get started, we'd like to offer you a **free copy** of one of our bestselling ebooks:

www.bkconnection.com/welcome

When you claim your **free ebook**, you'll also be subscribed to our blog.

Our freshest insights

Access the best new tools and ideas for leaders at all levels on our blog at ideas.bkconnection.com.

Sincerely,

Your friends at Berrett-Koehler

Certified

Corporation